Extreme Programming
in Practice

The XP Series

Kent Beck, Series Advisor

Extreme Programming, familiarly known as XP, is a discipline of business and software development that focuses both parties on common, reachable goals. XP teams produce quality software at a sustainable pace. The practices that make up "book" XP are chosen for their dependence on human creativity and acceptance of human frailty.

Although XP is often presented as a list of practices, XP is not a finish line. You don't get better and better grades at doing XP until you finally receive the coveted gold star. XP is a starting line. It asks the question, "How little can we do and still build great software?"

The beginning of the answer is that, if we want to leave software development uncluttered, we must be prepared to completely embrace the few practices we adopt. Half measures leave problems unsolved to be addressed by further half measures. Eventually you are surrounded by so many half measures that you can no longer see that the heart of the value programmers create comes from programming.

I say, "The beginning of the answer ..." because there is no final answer. The authors in the XP Series have been that and done there, and returned to tell their story. The books in this series are the signposts they have planted along the way: "Here lie dragons," "Scenic drive next 15 km," "Slippery when wet."

Excuse me, I gotta go program.

Titles in the Series

Extreme Programming Applied: Playing to Win, Ken Auer and Roy Miller

Extreme Programming Examined, Giancarlo Succi and Michele Marchesi

Extreme Programming Explained: Embrace Change, Kent Beck

Extreme Programming Explored, William C. Wake

Extreme Programming in Practice, James Newkirk and Robert C. Martin

Extreme Programming Installed, Ron Jeffries, Ann Anderson, and Chet Hendrickson

Planning Extreme Programming, Kent Beck and Martin Fowler

Extreme Programming
In Practice

James Newkirk
Robert C. Martin

ADDISON–WESLEY

Boston • San Francisco • New York • Toronto • Montreal
London • Munich • Paris • Madrid
Capetown • Sydney • Tokyo • Singapore • Mexico City

The publisher offers discounts on this book when ordered in quantity for special sales. For more information, please contact:

Pearson Education Corporate Sales Division
One Lake Street
Upper Saddle River, NJ 07458
(800) 382-3419
corpsales@pearsontechgroup.com

Visit us on the Web at www.awl.com/cseng/

ISBN 0-201-70937-6
Text printed on recycled paper
1 2 3 4 5 6 7 8 9—MA—0504030201
First printing, May 2001

Contents

List of User Stories

Foreword

—Martin Fowler

A large part of XP is about techniques that allow programmers to build simple and yet very flexible software. The key practices of testing, continuous integration, and refactoring combine to enable a design style that is more evolutionary than planned. This evolutionary design style is very important in the context of volatile requirements that is the world in which XP operates.

It's one thing to pass on these techniques in a mentoring environment, working with a group of developers; it's another, more challenging thing to boil these techniques down into book form.

In this book, Uncles Bob and Jim describe a very simple programming project. In many ways this project is too simple to draw any great conclusions from. However those of us who have done the XP style of programming can recognize in this small example much of the spirit of XP development. Enough of this spirit is here that I can say, "Work like this and you are taking the first crucial steps into the world of XP programming." And of course, if the example were any more complicated, it wouldn't fit into a book.

So if you're intrigued by XP, this gives you a small but representative example of what it feels like. If you try XP yourself, you will find new challenges, surprises, and delights. This book is a great launching pad.

Preface

This book is a case study describing a Web-based software project developed using a development process known as *Extreme Programming* (XP).[1] The project is real, driven by the needs of a real customer. The artifacts presented in this book are real. The code is real, the user stories are real, and the anecdotes are real. We videotaped all our meetings and development episodes so that we maintained an honest and objective chronicle of the events.[2] We wanted our readers to have as true-to-life an experience as possible.

At first we thought we might have to keep the scope of the project artificially small enough to fit into this book. However, it turned out that the size of the first XP release of the project was both useful to our customer and the ideal size for this book. So even the size of the release is real.

Before this project, none of us had used XP in its entirety. So this book also chronicles the adoption of XP by a team that is relatively unfamiliar with it.

---

1. Beck, K. 2000. *Extreme programming explained: Embrace change.* Reading, MA: Addison-Wesley.
2. Please don't ask for these tapes. The quality is poor, they are boring as hell, and they contain proprietary information.

Our goal in writing this book is to help demonstrate how a real XP project works. We have chosen to do this by example, rather than by explanation.

The examples are real. They chronicle the thought processes of the team as it struggles with the concepts of XP. You will see us make mistakes and then correct them. You will see us have insights and then find them to be invalid. You will see the ebb and flow of a real development project.

This book is written for developers, managers, customers, and anyone else involved in the development of software.

We welcome any feedback and can be reached at the following e-mail addresses:

✧ James Newkirk—jnewkirk@thoughtworks.com
✧ Robert C. Martin—rmartin@objectmentor.com

Acknowledgments

We'd like thank our customer, Lowell Lindstrom, for all his hard work and support. We'd also like to thank the following people: Chris Biegay and Micah Martin, who developed the last two iterations of our project; and Brian Button and James Grenning, who paired up with us on parts of the first iteration.

Our reviewers were Ann Anderson, Kent Beck, Paul Bouzide, Martin Fowler, Dave Hendricksen, Chet Hendrickson (it's his fault), Ron Jeffries (XpHammer), Jeff Langr, Andy Mather, Erik Meade, Paul Moore, James Nargi, Michael C. Two, Ross Walker, and Frank Westphal. We'd like to thank these folks for helping to improve this book. Any errors or omissions are our own and do not reflect on them in any way.

Thanks also to the fine folks at Addison-Wesley who helped us with editing, composition, and publishing. They are Mike Hendrickson, Heather Olszyk, Heather Peterson, Mamata Reddy, Beth Hayes, and Kim Arney Mulcahy.

Bob—I would like to thank my family for their forbearance and support for yet another project.

Jim—I would like to thank my family for their patience during the project and the subsequent writing of the book. Finally, I would also like to thank my friend and mentor, Robert Martin, for all his help throughout the years.

Chapter 1

The Skinny

I guess we should just shut it off until we
can free up some time to fix it.
—Lowell Lindstrom,
VP, Object Mentor, Inc.

The above quote is a sign of project failure. As is often the case the failure occurred on many fronts, technical as well as business. The most immediate concern is the lack of quality of the delivered software. It is not functioning as expected and is not delivering value to the business. How did the project get to this state?

Over the past couple of years, usage of our Web site has gone from a handful of people to over 6,000[1] hits a day, with about 300 unique sessions per day. Not Yahoo, but, for our niche in the marketplace, not bad. Our business depends on this Web site, because almost all of our customers find us on the Internet.

Most of the Web traffic is to access copies of articles that our employees have written. We also have a bookstore and a place to retrieve useful software utilities.

Our company provides training and mentoring to software developers who find our services on the Internet. To better understand who was using our services, why they valued our services, and how our Web site helped them become better software developers, we decided to keep track of Web usage. To begin with, we purchased a program that analyzed our Web server log files. This program produced statistics regarding Web usage and told us which topics were of most interest to our

---

1. At the time of this publication (June 2001), it had grown to 16,000.

customers. However, the program was not capable of telling us much about who our users were. Oh sure, we got some feedback about specific companies, but our biggest usage was from a big Internet service provider in Virginia.[2]

We also had users who had asked to be notified when new articles became available. We considered this a good way to keep in contact with current and potential customers.

It was clear we needed some kind of user registration mechanism. Many Web sites like ours were already using such mechanisms; however, these mechanisms were often intrusive and annoying. Our company prides itself on being a good Internet citizen, so our registration mechanism had to be as unobtrusive as possible.

The First Solution

We found several sites that shared our minimalist philosophy. We wanted a mechanism to have users log in before being able to download the articles and applications. We called this our *registration system*. Using some simple Web page layout tools, we worked up a prototype that seemed to meet our needs.

We were in a hurry to get this working, so we cobbled together some active server pages (ASP) and JavaScript code, borrowing heavily from books and examples on the Web. We used Microsoft Access through ODBC to store the registration data. This turned out to be a straightforward process.

Initially, the project was a big success, aside from a few complaints from users who viewed registration as a mild distraction. Most users requested to be notified of modifications, and our usage traffic continued to grow. As a result we had better information to develop the Web site to meet the needs of users.

Changes

Our Web server was also our mail, contact, and calendar server, so the server environment changed whenever we adjusted any of these services. In the process of making one of these seemingly unrelated changes, the registration system silently stopped working.

---

2. America Online is based in Reston, Virginia.

The failure must have occurred when we downloaded and installed a new calendar manager on the server. The installation somehow corrupted some of the system ODBC data source names. This caused the registration of new users to fail, preventing them from accessing our site. We didn't know this at first, because the ASP scripts that accessed the database were not reporting errors in a way that we could immediately see.

Unable to log in, our users started sending us nasty messages:

> *This sucks because now I can't get to the material that I want to read. Please fix and let me know when it is working.*
>
> —*Allan Vermeulen, VP, Amazon.com*

The registration system went from being a mild distraction to blocking access to the most valued resources at the site. A critical business system was suddenly a deterrent to new customers.

> *I guess we should just shut it off until we can free up some time to fix it.*
>
> —*Lowell Lindstrom, VP, Object Mentor, Inc.*

What Went Wrong?

We were in a hurry; we threw some code together, and we got it working. In truth, we were doing it more for fun than for its direct business value. We wanted to learn about ASP and COM, we wanted to play around with Web software, and we figured we'd get some business value at the same time. We didn't think about employing a process.

We were lucky. The failure we experienced had no appreciable effect on our business. But it might have been worse. Once the program failed, we realized that simply fixing it was not the best option. A lot was at stake, and future failures could significantly harm our business. We realized we needed to employ a process for making changes to our Web site. In hindsight: Duh.

Chapter 2

Playing to Win

If we must use a development process, we want it to be one that is agile, aggressive, and pragmatic. We want it to help us understand the requirements and produce software that meets those requirements. We want it to impose no delays and to help us to go as fast as we can without sacrificing quality. When problems occur, we want the process to help us repair them instead of helping us to assign blame. We want to play to win.

Extreme Programming (XP)

For many years, we had been using an ad hoc set of development values that was iterative, lightweight, and aggressive. We valued human communication over paper, valued good code over good diagrams, valued quick iterations with customer feedback, and valued up-front software design to manage dependencies. We'd had a lot of success with these values, but they were far from a written process definition.

In 1998, we heard about Kent Beck's work with Extreme Programming (XP), and we studied it carefully. XP resonated with many of our values, but challenged some others. XP values human communications over paper, values good code over diagrams, values quick iterations with customer feedback, and values evolutionary design over up-front design.

The similarity in values was compelling, and we wanted to try it. But the up-front design dilemma was disturbing. One way to confront this dilemma might have been to accept some of the XP practices and dismiss others. We could have tried to merge up-front design with XP. However, we had quite a bit of experience with evolving designs and had also had some failures involving up-front design.[1] So it was not hard for us to suspend our disbelief regarding up-front design and simply try XP.

So, we decided to employ XP as the process for developing the registration system for our Web site.

The Structure of This Book

✦ What is XP?
  — A brief overview of XP practices and principles used in this book

✦ Exploration
  — The story of a story
  — Combining stories
  — Architecture
  — Legacy conversion
  — Estimating stories

✦ Planning the first release
  — How the customer decided what stories would go into our first release
  — Prioritizing the stories
  — The priority of architectural significance
  — Velocity, iteration length, and release duration

✦ Iteration 1 planning
  — Breaking stories into tasks
  — Signing up for tasks
  — Task estimation
  — Task estimates don't match story estimates

---

1. Martin, R. C., and J. W. Newkirk. 1995. "A case study of OOD and reuse in C++." *Object Magazine*. 1995.

Chapter 3

What Is XP?

*XP is a lightweight methodology for small- to
medium-sized teams developing software in the
face of vague or rapidly changing requirements.*
—Kent Beck[1]

Introduction

An XP project begins with a period of exploration. The purpose of
exploration is to identify, prioritize, and estimate requirements. Once
enough requirements have been identified to provide the smallest system that will yield value to the customer, the first release is planned.
Over time, further explorations will yield more requirements and other
releases will be planned.

Releases are broken down into several iterations. Software is written
in each iteration, and each iteration delivers something of value to the
customer.

Exploration

Exploration takes the place of a written requirements document. The
programmers and the customer[2] assemble and discuss the customer's
needs. The customer writes stories describing these needs. In discussion

---

1. Beck, K. 2000. *Extreme programming explained: Embrace change*. Reading, MA:
   Addison-Wesley.
2. If you have more than one customer, they still must speak with a single voice.

with the customer, the programmers remove ambiguity from the stories by making sure that they are testable and estimable. Customers make sure that stories are meaningful by ordering them in terms of their business value.

Stories are typically written on index cards. They do not contain a lot of text. Rather, they act as reminders of the conversations between the programmers and the customer. Later on, during each iteration, the customer provides written detail about the stories in the form of acceptance tests.

Story estimates are written on the cards and are provided solely by the programmers. They are given in arbitrary units of effort and are proportional to the amount of time a task will take. Some programmers use *ideal programming weeks*.[3]

A story must to be small enough for the team to develop within an iteration (one to three weeks). Smaller stories are better than larger ones. A story must be testable. The customer should be able to specify acceptance tests that verify that the story is correct and complete. Passing these tests is the definition of being finished. Finally, the customer must be able to assign a priority to each story. A story should have a single responsibility that carries a single priority. If parts of a story are more important than other parts, the story should be split into two or more smaller stories.

Spike

During exploration, or any time the team needs to resolve uncertainty or mitigate risk, they can conduct a spike. A *spike* is a very fast experiment that drives deep into the issue in question. For example, if you've never sent e-mail from a servlet before, you probably will not be able to estimate how long it will take. So instead of guessing, you run a spike. You write throw-away code that proves you can send that e-mail. Then you'll be able to estimate the real task.

---

3. An *ideal programming week* is the amount of work you can complete in a week during which the phone does not ring, there are no meetings, you don't have to work with anyone else, nobody bugs you, you aren't sick, you don't have a hangover, you don't get hungry, you are always alert, and you see pigs fly.

Release Planning

An XP project is broken up into a series of releases. Each release will provide business value to the customer. When planning a release the customer selects the stories that will be implemented. This selection might not be the most technically efficient, but it ensures that each release provides the most value to the business. Business value overrides technical efficiency.

A release usually takes one to three months. The shorter the release, the quicker we get feedback. However, a release must also provide value to the business, and the business must be able to absorb the value. In the end the customer decides how long the release will be.

When planning a release, there is a simple rule to follow. The team cannot commit to doing more work than they did in the previous release. This work is measured in terms of the estimates written on the story cards. The sum of these numbers in a release is known as the *release velocity*. For the first release the team chooses a reasonable but arbitrary[4] velocity.

Most projects anchor the duration of the release and choose stories to fit. Other projects may choose several stories and adjust the duration; however, this often leads to longer releases, which can be difficult to manage.

This technique delineates the responsibility between the customer and the programmers. The customer decides the content. The programmers provide estimates. Velocity is simply the amount of work done in the previous release. The customer is not allowed to influence the estimates, programmers are not allowed to change the content, and no one second-guesses the velocity.

Iteration Planning

A release is broken up into several one- to three-week iterations. The iteration length is chosen at the beginning of the project and remains constant thereafter.

The team starts planning the iteration by giving the customer a budget. This budget is the amount of work that the developers think they can get done. This number is given in the same units as the story estimates.

---

4. "Arbitrary" because it is not based on measured data.

Once again a simple rule applies: The amount of work developers can commit to in an iteration is the same as the amount they finished in the last iteration. For the first iteration a reasonable but arbitrary estimate is provided. It will be wrong, but subsequent iterations will correct it rapidly.

The customer chooses the stories that will be completely implemented in the iteration and agrees not to change or add to them until the iteration is complete. The customer also specifies acceptance tests that indicate successful completion of the stories.

The programmers break the stories down into tasks and determine the order in which to implement them. Tasks should be no longer than a day or two in duration.

Tasks are not assigned; programmers sign up for the ones on which they want to work. No tasks can remain unchosen. Programmers estimate the tasks that they signed up for by considering what they completed in the last iteration. Programmers are not allowed to be responsible for more tasks than they completed in the last iteration, so rebalancing may be necessary.

The estimates are summed and compared with the duration of the iteration. If there is too much work to do, the customer decides what will be moved from this iteration to the next. The customer may move entire stories or partial stories to a future iteration. If the estimates don't fill the iteration, the customer supplies more stories.

Once again there is a delineation of responsibility. Customers choose content (stories) and specify completion criteria (acceptance tests). Programmers provide estimates and choose implementation strategy.

Development

Though individual programmers have taken responsibility for the tasks, all production software is written by *pairs* of programmers. Each pair works at a single workstation, sharing the keyboard.

Pairs typically break up after a few hours, and different pairs form. Pairs form when one programmer asks another for help. The rule is: When asked, you can't say no. However, if you give help, it is fair to expect help in return.

Software is developed one test case at a time. The pair decides what part of a task to work on and designs a test case to verify it. Then the pair writes the code that passes that test case. When the test case passes, they move on to the next test case.

These test/develop episodes are very small, usually five to ten minutes. They continue until all the test cases for a task have been written and pass.

The tests are just as important as the production code. They are gathered together into a unit testing harness and are run every time the code is changed. All the tests must pass both before and after the code is integrated into the main system. In practice, programmers run the tests frequently to make sure they haven't inadvertently broken something. The programmers follow simple rules:

- ✧ Programmers do not anticipate future stories or features. They write only the code that is needed to complete the current task.

- ✧ Programmers practice frequent *refactoring*[5] in order to keep the code as clean and simple as possible. Duplication is not allowed in the code. When found, it is removed by creating the necessary abstractions.

- ✧ Integration is done as frequently as possible, at least once per day and often more frequently.

- ✧ Programers do not own the code they write or modify. Any pair can check out and modify any module for any reason.

- ✧ Programmers maintain a sustainable rate of effort. They are not allowed to work two or more weeks of overtime in a row.

---

5. Fowler, M. 1999. *Refactoring: Improving the design of existing code*. Reading, MA: Addison-Wesley.

Chapter 4

Exploration

*To search into or travel in for the
purpose of discovery*
—Dictionary.com

We sat down with Lowell, our customer, and started to explore what he wanted the registration system to do. Over the next two days we wound up with several user stories. Though these user stories described the system nicely, the mechanism by which they were generated was not at all straightforward.

The Story of a Story

For example, our first user story slowly evolved into what is shown in User Story 4.1: *Triggering the Login Mechanism.*

The three phrases on this story were written at three different times by three different people. The first phrase was written by Lowell in response to our question: "When do you want users to have to log in?"

We couldn't figure out how to test this. What acceptance test would you write? We needed more information about which pages would trigger login and which wouldn't. But Lowell was not willing to be specific about this.

Eventually we decided that there would have to be a list somewhere in the system that told us which pages required a login. When those pages were requested by a user, the login mechanism would be triggered.

15

USER STORY 4.1 Triggering the Login Mechanism

We felt comfortable about testing this, because we could create lists and see if the mechanism was triggered. We also felt comfortable that the story was estimable. So, somebody scribbled the second phrase on the story card.

At some point much later in the discussion and after many other user stories had been discussed, somebody asked whether or not users would have to log in every time they requested one of the pages on the list. Lowell felt this would be awful. So, after some discussion, we decided to create the concept of a session that represented an interaction with our site and that would conclude after the user had been silent for x minutes. Users would not need to log in more than once per session. Someone wrote the last phrase on the card.

Much later, we estimated our stories and felt this one could be implemented in one ideal engineering day.

The Story of Some Constraints

While we were talking about User Story 4.1: *Triggering the Login Mechanism*, someone suggested that the login should pop up in a separate window. Lowell's eyes filled with fear, and he quickly scribbled down User Story 4.2: *No Pop-Up Windows*.

This is an interesting story because this function cannot be implemented by a direct action. Rather, it is a constraint that must be obeyed, and thus it cannot be directly estimated.

Another such constraint is shown in User Story 4.3: *Username as E-mail Address*. The previous system had generated a unique username

```
The system will not pop up a window that could be inter-
preted as a pop-up ad.




Constraint
```

USER STORY 4.2 No Pop-Up Windows

for each new user. Users were having trouble remembering these
names. So Lowell decided that the user's e-mail address was a good,
unique username. This has become common at other sites.

The constraint in User Story 4.4: *Porting Constraint* came about
because Lowell wanted to preserve a migration path from Windows NT
to Linux. In the previous system, we had been using ASP on Windows
NT. But Lowell was beginning to think that a Linux server might be
better. There were no immediate plans for porting, but Lowell didn't
want to prevent the port either. So, Lowell decided that we should not
make it hard to port to Linux. Programmers can interpret something
such as this in several ways. We could ignore it and wait until it became
an actual story, and then we could estimate the effort. Or we could use
this bit of information to choose between what might be seen as equal

```
The username should be an e-mail address.




Constraint
```

USER STORY 4.3 Username as E-mail Address

USER STORY 4.4 Porting Constraint

implementation choices. In fact, active content for the site could be provided by ASP or Java Server Pages (JSP) and Java Servlets. Given this information, we decided to use JSP and Java Servlets for the member area of the site. We wouldn't change everything right away, but we also wouldn't add any more ASP.

Words of the Customer

Customer Picks the Operating System?

One of the aims of XP is to have the technical team make the technical decisions and the business team make the business decisions. The choice of operating system (OS) would seem to be one for the technical team to make. In this case the tasks required to support the Windows NT server were becoming a drain on our resources and delaying progress on other projects. We have UNIX and Linux skills on staff, so the move to Linux has business value.

Architecture

A servlet-based system looks something like the diagram in Figure 4.1. Client workstations, using Web browsers, access our server over the Internet. Our server serves pages that contain servlet URLs. Those servlets execute on the server and generate HTML that is sent along with the

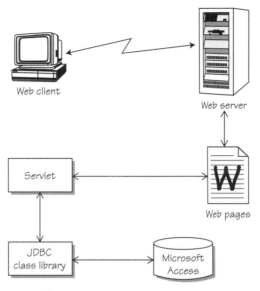

FIGURE 4.1 System architecture

pages. The servlets draw their data from and manipulate a Microsoft Access database.

The simple model in Figure 4.1 is sufficient to be able to generate estimates of the stories. We can see where those stories fit and judge how much effort they will require.

An Expensive Story

Many of the stories fit nicely into the existing active server page implementation, so it was not necessary to convert the entire Web site to servlets. Our intention was to write only the registration system in servlets.

However, Lowell wrote one user story that was much more complicated. User Story 4.5: *Smart Site Header* affects every page. To implement it, we either had to write a lot more ASP code or change every page to servlets and JSPs.

The site header is the banner that appears on all our Web pages. It gives our pages a consistent look and feel, and provides common navigation links to the other parts of our site. Lowell wanted a small icon to

The site header (i.e., on all pages) should indicate if the user
has not logged in and offer them a button to log in (similar to
a shopping cart). Show name or e-mail if logged in.

Five days

USER STORY 4.5 Smart Site Header

appear in this header if the user had not logged in. Clicking on that
icon would trigger the login mechanism. If the user was logged in, the
icon would show the user's e-mail address or name if he or she had
given it to us.

The estimate on this story is high—five perfect days—because it
would force us to remove the ASP code from every page in the system
and replace it with JSPs or servlets.

Combining Stories

As we began talking about how users log in, Lowell wrote User
Story 4.6: *Login Story*. During the discussion, this story brought forth

When the login is triggered, and the site cannot detect that
the user is a member, the user is transferred to a login page,
which asks for their username and password and explains
the login process & philosophy of the site.

Two days

USER STORY 4.6 Login Story

USER STORY 4.7 Cookies

several issues. For example, how would we know whether the user was already a member? If users are already members, do they need to log in or would we log them in automatically? Lastly, should we allow access to people who do not want to become members?

The answer to the first question, how we know whether the user is already a member, turned out to be straightforward: We could store a "cookie" in the user's browser. However, some users do not allow server sites to store cookies. So Lowell wrote User Story 4.7: *Cookies*, to allow the user to select whether or not a cookie would be stored.

For some people the login process is a distraction. Lowell wanted to allow people to bypass the login and still have access to the site without the benefits of membership. So he wrote User Story 4.8: *Guest Login*, which allows users the ability to log in as a guest.

The login window must allow the user to skip the login, which logs them in as a guest.

USER STORY 4.8 Guest Login

When the login mechanism is triggered and the person is already a member, detectable by the site, the person is sent to the page that they requested.

"TRANSPARENT"

USER STORY 4.9 Transparent Login

Finally, Lowell did not want users who had already registered, and who had allowed us to write a cookie, to have to log in every time they visited our site. So, he wrote User Story 4.9: *Transparent Login.*

During these discussions, we started drawing a picture of what the login screen might look like. This picture evolved as shown in Figure 4.2. This picture captures all the issues in the four previous user stories, so we clipped them all together with a paperclip and estimated them as a single user story.

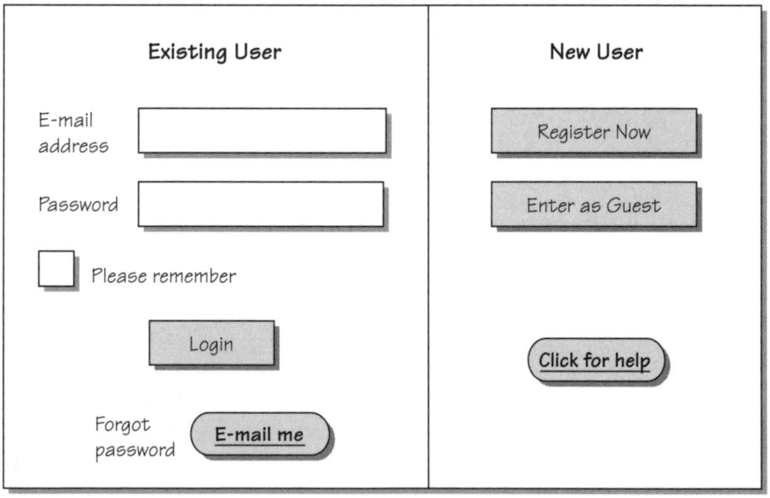

FIGURE 4.2 Create member page

Registration Story

User Story 4.9: *Transparent Login* opened the door to discussions about what we would like from users in terms of registration information. We definitely needed a unique identifier for each person. User Story 4.3: *Username as E-mail Address,* on page 17, describes a constraint that we can now satisfy by turning it into a story. We will use the e-mail address as the unique identifier. Because we intend to use the e-mail address to keep interested users informed, we must verify that it is valid. To do this, we will send a system-created password to the specified e-mail address.

In addition, we will request first and last names, professional affiliation (i.e., company, college, etc.), and whether or not the user wants to be notified of changes to the site.

This discussion yielded User Story 4.10: *User Registration.*

To estimate this story, we had to perform a spike to test the feasibility and difficulty of e-mailing from a servlet. On the Internet, we found several Java class libraries intended for this purpose. We spent a couple of hours downloading and trying one of them. This proved straightforward and made us feel comfortable estimating the story.

Existing User

As the conversation continued, we began to wonder what would happen if someone entered an e-mail address that was already registered in the system. For User Story 4.11: *Existing User*, Lowell decided that in this case the user had forgotten that he or she was a member. He

---

When the user selects to register, they should be taken to the registration page, which prompts the user for an e-mail address, first name, last name, affiliation, and whether or not they want to be notified of changes to the site. Upon submit, the system generates a password and e-mails it to the user.

E-mail field must be nonblank.

Two days

USER STORY 4.10 User Registration

> If during registration, the user enters an e-mail address that already exists, a page should ask them if the site should send their password to them
>
> One day

USER STORY 4.11 Existing User

> If the user selects "forgot password," they should be prompted to enter the e-mail address that they registered with and the password will be e-mailed to that address, within 15 seconds
>
> One day

USER STORY 4.12 Forgotten Password

---

decided to send the user's password just as though the user was registering for the first time. In User Story 4.12: *Forgotten Password*, the user knows that he or she is already a member; the user simply has forgotten his or her password.

Legacy Conversion

Lowell wanted the members from the old registration system, as well as some e-mail addresses gathered over the years, to become members of the new registration system. This required two activities. The first was to inform the old members via e-mail of the changes to the regis-

Migrate old Microsoft Access data to new system.
— Send e-mail to users confirming their memberships

One day

USER STORY 4.13 Migrate Access Data

Migrate legacy e-mail addresses to members.

Send e-mail to confirm membership with their password.

Inform how to easily cancel if not interested.

Three days

USER STORY 4.14 Legacy E-mail Addresses

tration system (User Story 4.13: *Migrate Access Data*). The next time that they visited our site they would need to log in. The second activity was to automatically register several hundred e-mail addresses and send the users their new passwords (User Story 4.14: *Legacy E-mail Addresses*).

Notification

Lowell wanted it to be easy for customers to request notification, and he also thought it might be better if the customers were specific about topics they wanted to be notified about. He also wanted it to be easy

> I (marketing guy) need the ability to send the same e-mail to all members that have checked the box for notification [no mail merge functionality].
>
>
>
> One day

USER STORY 4.15 E-mail Notification

> The customer should be able to register to be notified when classes/papers/schedules/offerings change.
>
> Little check boxes for each category.
>
>
>
> One day

USER STORY 4.16 Notification Specialization

---

for him to notify them. User Story 4.15: *E-mail Notification* and User Story 4.16: *Notification Specialization* describe these activities.

Appearance of Registration Pages

The site currently restricts page width to 600 pixels. This was a common convention for Web pages when the site was designed. During the discussion of the registration system, Lowell said he wanted the registration pages to look good even if the window was larger than 600 pixels. He then wrote User Story 4.17: *Page Width*.

Miscellaneous

The following two user stories (User Story 4.18: *Member Invitation* and User Story 4.19: *Changing User Profile*) came about as part of the overall discussion and do not need much additional explanation.

Variable-width HTML pages.

Two days

USER STORY 4.17 Page Width

Provide a facility to allow users to invite other people to become a member (by sending them an HTML form). Upon receiving a reply the system registers them and sends a confirming e-mail with their password.

Three days

USER STORY 4.18 Member Invitation

Users must be able to change their profile (e-mail address, password, first name, last name, affiliation).

Two passwords fields for confirmation.

Two days

USER STORY 4.19 Changing User Profile

Conclusion

This discussion took place over two days and did not take place in the order presented here. In fact, the stories were produced in a random way by discussions that led to other discussions and back again.

This is a topic that Lowell and the programmers (Jim and Bob) were very familiar with, so much of the context described in these pages remained unspoken between them. In fact, a fly on the wall would have heard a group of people speaking in broken sentences, grunts, and moans, each finishing the others' thoughts. Most people watching the videotapes would not understand what was happening.

Summary of Stories

Table 4.1 is a summary of the user stories and their estimates.

TABLE 4.1 Story Estimates

Story	Estimate (ideal days)
User Story 4.1: *Triggering the Login Mechanism*	1
User Story 4.2: *No Pop-Up Windows*	0
User Story 4.3: *Username as E-mail Address*	0
User Story 4.4: *Porting Constraint*	0
User Story 4.5: *Smart Site Header*	5
User Story 4.6: *Login Story* User Story 4.7: *Cookies* User Story 4.8: *Guest Login* User Story 4.9: *Transparent Login*	2
User Story 4.10: *User Registration*	2
User Story 4.11: *Existing User*	1
User Story 4.12: *Forgotten Password*	1
User Story 4.13: *Migrate Access Data*	1
User Story 4.14: *Legacy E-mail Addresses*	3
User Story 4.15: *E-mail Notification*	1
User Story 4.16: *Notification Specialization*	1
User Story 4.17: *Page Width*	2
User Story 4.18: *Member Invitation*	3
User Story 4.19: *Changing User Profile*	2
Total	25

Chapter 5

Planning

The best laid schemes o' mice and men
Gang aft a-gley,
And leave us naught but grief and pain for promised joy.
—Robert Burns (1759–1796)

The exploration described in Chapter 4 yielded more than 25 days' worth of work. This was more than enough stories for the first release. There were many other things the system could and should do. Some methods recommend continuing exploration until all primary system features have been identified. This allows system architects to design a system with full knowledge of its features, or so the argument goes.

However, often when a customer sees the system for the first time, he or she realizes that the requested features are not the features really desired. If we were to explore all the features of the system, the customer would likely change many of them upon seeing the first release. Therefore, once we have enough stories to make a release, it is more efficient to slow exploration and start developing.

Developing the first release before all features have been explored will likely mean that the first release will have to be reworked because its design will not be consistent with all the features. This sounds like a reason to wait. However, we don't trust the features. Customers are going to change the features when they first see the system or when the business environment changes. If we invest a lot of effort in designing the full set of features, we will have to rework a lot more than if we stop exploring and build the release for the features we have.

TABLE 5.1 Prioritized Stories

Immediate	Short-term wait	Long-term wait
User Story 4.2: *No Pop-Up Windows*	User Story 4.1: *Triggering the Login Mechanism*	User Story 4.14: *Legacy E-mail Addresses*
User Story 4.3: *Username as E-mail Address*	User Story 4.5: *Smart Site Header*	User Story 4.16: *Notification Specialization*
User Story 4.6: *Login Story*	User Story 4.13: *Migrate Access Data*	User Story 4.17: *Page Width*
User Story 4.7: *Cookies*	User Story 4.19: *Changing User Profile*	User Story 4.18: *Member Invitation*
User Story 4.8: *Guest Login*		User Story 4.4: *Porting Constraint*
User Story 4.9: *Transparent Login*		
User Story 4.10: *User Registration*		
User Story 4.11: *Existing User*		
User Story 4.12: *Forgotten Password*		
User Story 4.15: *E-mail Notification*		

Prioritizing the Stories

Lowell took the stories and arranged them into three piles (see Table 5.1). The first pile contained stories he wanted to see implemented immediately. The second pile contained stories for which he was willing to wait a short time. The third pile were stories for which he was willing to wait a long time.

Architectural Significance

User Story 4.5: *Smart Site Header* has a lot of architectural significance. The programmers would prefer to do this one first. However,

Lowell did not consider this story to be a high priority. Thus it had to wait until a later iteration.

Deferring architecturally significant features may sound risky, but so is investing architectural energy in a feature that may never be implemented. It is better to deal with architecture when the architecture is needed than to implement it early and wait until it is needed.

Release and Iteration Duration

We chose an iteration duration of one week and a release duration of three iterations. This choice was arbitrary. We wanted short iterations so that we could get rapid feedback from Lowell. We wanted the release to be large enough to contain the minimum set of stories that Lowell thought were needed to go live.

Not every project can ship on a three-week release schedule. There are deployment, distribution, documentation, and Q/A issues that make it convenient to have longer release times. However, our project is a Web site, so most of these barriers are insignificant. A three-week release cycle is convenient and gets the system in front of real users as quickly as possible.

Velocity

Having no data to draw upon, we conservatively chose individual velocities of 2.5 (i.e., we each thought we could do 2.5 ideal engineering days of work in a five-day iteration). This means that a user story estimated at three ideal days would consume six calendar days. Since there were two programmers working on the project, our team velocity was five ($2 \times 2.5 = 5$). So a three-ideal-day user story should require three calendar days.

We don't expect that this choice of velocity is accurate, so the first iteration is unlikely to go as planned. However, we intend to track our true velocity during the first iteration and use that as the basis for planning the second iteration.

Planning the First Release

Armed with the priorities, estimates, and velocity, Lowell was ready to determine the contents of the first release. He began by summing the estimates for the immediate and short-term tasks. This came to 16 ideals days.

In true customer fashion, Lowell asked that the release be extended by one day. We told him that we didn't want to do this, because it was unlikely that our velocity and estimates were accurate. We felt it would be better to keep the iterations and releases regular so we could measure our progress.

A three-week release has 15 working days. Two of us, working at an assumed velocity of 2.5, ought to be able to finish 15 ideal days in 15 real days. So, Lowell had to remove one ideal day from the release.

Up to this point, Lowell had assumed that he would get all the stories implemented before the system went live. However, the total of the story estimates exceeded the 15 days allotted for the release. So, faced with putting the system live with a partial set of stories, Lowell questioned the priorities he had assigned.

User Story 4.16: *Notification Specialization*, caught his eye. To launch the system, we were going to have to send e-mails out to all our old users (User Story 4.13: *Migrate Access Data*). If *Notification Specialization* was not implemented by then, the users would not be able to specify what they were interested in. Then, once *Notification Specialization* was finally implemented, we'd have to send another batch of e-mails to tell the users to set their interests. Lowell felt this would be a nuisance, so he moved *Notification Specialization* into the release.

Now we had 17 ideal days in the release, and Lowell had to shed two days instead of one. He chose to delete User Story 4.1: *Triggering the Login Mechanism*, the story that forced a user to log in when first coming to the site. His reasoning was that if User Story 4.5: *Smart Site Header*, was implemented, users would be continuously reminded to log in and would not need to be coerced. Also, the fact that *Notification Specialization* allows users to specify the things that they want to be notified about gives users a reason to want to log in.

The other story that Lowell removed from the release was User Story 4.11: *Existing User*. Pulling this story meant that existing users who were reregistering because they had forgotten they already had an account would suffer some inconvenience. Instead of being automatically routed to the screen to request a forgotten password, they would get an error message stating that their account could not be added. Even though this story was of the highest priority, Lowell felt that its loss was acceptable.

After about 30 minutes of discussion over these issues, the release was finalized as follows:

- ✧ User Story 4.6: *Login Story*
- ✧ User Story 4.7: *Cookies*
- ✧ User Story 4.8: *Guest Login*
- ✧ User Story 4.9: *Transparent Login*
- ✧ User Story 4.12: *Forgotten Password*
- ✧ User Story 4.15: *E-mail Notification*
- ✧ User Story 4.10: *User Registration*
- ✧ User Story 4.19: *Changing User Profile*
- ✧ User Story 4.13: *Migrate Access Data*
- ✧ User Story 4.5: *Smart Site Header*
- ✧ User Story 4.16: *Notification Specialization*

Conclusion

Clearly, Lowell's interpretation of priority changed when faced with putting a partial system live. Just as clearly, it was the estimates on the stories that allowed Lowell to select the most important stories for the release. We, the programmers, participated by clarifying issues when Lowell was confused, explaining the repercussions of Lowell's decisions, and standing by our estimates and defending the release schedule.

Chapter 6

The First Iteration Plan

Man plans and God laughs.
—Hebrew Proverb

Now that we had our first release planned, it was time to plan the first iteration of that release. It is during iteration planning that programmers take control of the planning process from the customer. This transition of control occurs gradually as more and more technical issues drive the growing plan.

Lowell knew that each iteration was five days in duration. So he had to choose five days' worth of stories. Lowell sorted through the stories that were planned for the release, and passed six cards to us. He chose User Story 4.10: *User Registration*, User Story 4.6: *Login Story*, User Story 4.7: *Cookies*, User Story 4.8: *Guest Login*, User Story 4.9: *Transparent Login*, and User Story 4.12: *Forgotten Password*.

This way of selecting what should be worked on first is often criticized because it does not address architectural risk. For example, what if the stories that Lowell gave us caused us to create an infrastructure that was not suitable for future stories?

However, our iteration is only one week long. What damage can we do in a week? We just can't create that much infrastructure in a week. So, if we find we have to change it later, we won't be changing very much.

Breaking Stories into Tasks

At this point, we (Bob and Jim) started discussing the technical breakdown of the stories into tasks. Lowell asked us what he should be doing. We suggested that he could go get us something to eat, because this was likely to take some time. He asked if he could play any other role. We told him that it would be good to have him around if we had any questions, but that didn't have to be his primary focus. So he went to go get us some food (it was his house after all).

We began with User Story 4.6: *Login Story*, User Story 4.7: *Cookies*, User Story 4.8: *Guest Login*, and User Story 4.9: *Transparent Login*. We had a discussion about how the user would log in and what to do if the user already had a cookie. We talked for a long time about what would happen if a user was using someone else's computer and was logged in with someone else's cookie. We thought it might be a good idea to put a button on the login acknowledgment window asking if the user wanted to log in as someone else. (See Task 6.1.)

By this time, Lowell had arrived with pretzels, soda, popcorn, and chips. We drew a simple picture of the login screen and made the second task the creation of the HTML for that screen. (See Task 6.2.)

After a short break and a few phone calls, we began working on the login task. This task contains the logic of the login servlet. This servlet checks whether or not the e-mail address and password entered by the

Login Start

Read cookie.
If present
    Display login acknowledgment with user e-mail address
        and option to blow away cookie and log in as
        someone else.
else
    Bring up login page

TASK 6.1 Login Start

TASK 6.2 Login Page HTML

user are registered in the database. If they are and if the user allows, the servlet stores a cookie in the user's browser and routes to the requested page. If the e-mail and password don't exist or don't match, then no cookie is stored, and the user is routed to a login failure page. (See Task 6.3.)

Login Task

Takes data from HTML input. Checks the database for e-mail and password. Stores cookie if selection has been made. Routes to URL from where you came from if successful. Creates session (allow per-session cookie). If not successful, back to login with message indicating failure.

TASK 6.3 Login Task

After a few more phone calls, we started talking about how the login servlet would treat guests. Our goal was to create the least amount of annoyance for the user. On the login page, there is a button asking users to log in as a guest. If they push this button, they are anonymously logged in and have full access to the site for that session. Of course, guests cannot be put on our mailing list or receive notification about new offerings. (See Task 6.4.)

Next we started talking about users who forgot their password. This comes from User Story 4.12: *Forgotten Password*. Users can hit the "Forgot password" button on the login page and be taken to a page where they can enter their e-mail address and have their password e-mailed to them. (See Task 6.5.)

Next, we started talking about User Story 4.10: *User Registration*, and realized that we had neglected to create a task to create the database in Microsoft Access. This task is a simple enumeration of the fields we thought we needed for each user record. (See Task 6.6.)

The fields are standard. The notification field for this iteration is a Boolean variable. The user can simply select whether or not to be notified about new services. Other stories, not selected for this iteration, allow the user to select different categories of services to be notified about. It would be really easy to put something in the database about these categories. We know we are going to need them, and we have a pretty good idea of what they are about.

> ### Enter as Guest Task
>
> Creates a session with user as guest and goes to the requested page.

TASK 6.4 Enter as Guest Task

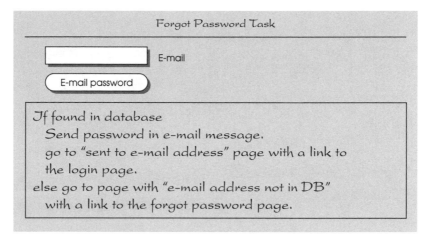

TASK 6.5 Forgot Password Task

For example, we could put a string in the database and use comma-separated values to specify the categories of interest to the user. This would cost very little now and would pave the way for what we know to be a future feature.

This was tempting, but we decided not to do it. We felt it was better to do the simplest thing to make the iteration work. If Lowell still wants notification categories by the time the next iteration comes

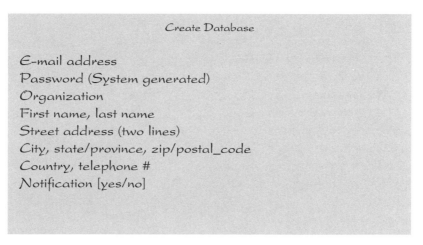

TASK 6.6 Create Database Task

Registration HTML

HTML for registration form. Button on form takes you to the Registration Servlet.

TASK 6.7 Registration HTML

around, we can add them then. We don't need to pollute this iteration with something that isn't necessary for it.

So, we continued our discussion of User Story 4.10: *User Registration*. We decided to create a task for the HTML of the registration page and another story for the logic of the registration servlet. (See Task 6.7 and Task 6.8.)

Task 6.8 is particularly interesting. It seems to assume that User Story 4.11: *Existing User* is in the iteration. Remember, the discussion

Registration Task Servlet

Pull data from HTML input.
If e-mail present in database
    go to "forgot password" screen.
else
    Generate password.
    Insert user into database.
    E-mail password to e-mail then go to login screen.

TASK 6.8 Registration Task Servlet

on page 32? Lowell had removed *Existing User* from the release. Yet here it is being implemented in Task 6.8. Clearly, our familiarity with the story cards had led us to include a story that should have been removed. Lowell, who was sitting right with us, was on the phone, so he didn't notice. It's not clear that he would have said anything anyway, being just as familiar with the stories as we were.

It turns out, as you will see in later chapters, that we never implemented this part of Task 6.8. It's not clear why. As we started implementing the system, we started to understand it better. As we saw the screens, it became clear what really needed to happen.

We can conclude from this that minor errors in release and task planning are not critical. First, the iterations are short, so the magnitude of the error can never be great. More importantly, the system is self-correcting. As you see the system start to work, you have a better appreciation for what it must do. Thus the end of an iteration may not be what was envisioned at the start. Clearly, the customer must be a part of this.

Signing Up for Tasks

Once the task breakdown is complete, the programmers take responsibility for individual tasks by signing up for them. Jim signed up for all the login-related tasks and the creation of the database. Bob signed up for the registration task, forgot password, and enter as guest. (See Table 6.1.)

Because there were only two of us, we worked together on the tasks. So the act of signing up did not turn out to be as important as it might

TABLE 6.1 Task Signup Table for Iteration 1

Task	Programmer
Task 6.1: *Login Start*	Jim
Task 6.2: *Login Page HTML*	Jim
Task 6.3: *Login Task*	Jim
Task 6.4: *Enter as Guest Task*	Bob
Task 6.5: *Forgot Password Task*	Bob
Task 6.6: *Create Database Task*	Jim
Task 6.7: *Registration HTML*	Bob
Task 6.8: *Registration Task Servlet*	Bob

appear here. When there are more than two people, signing up becomes more significant.

Estimating the Tasks

As we began to estimate these tasks, we realized the estimates must include the time spent writing tests for the tasks. So we spent a bit of time simply trying to understand the kinds of tests we'd have to write.

The first task we considered was Task 6.6: *Create Database Task*. We talked about how to test insertion and deletion of users, how to test that the right fields were present and had the right types, and so on. Jim felt that it would take one ideal day to create all the tests and write the code that passed the tests.

Had we not been thinking about the tests, had we just considered how long it would take to build a database, we would have estimated this at much less than a day. Thinking about the tests forced us to work through some of the design issues and gave us a better idea of the complexity of the task.

Next we estimated Task 6.1: *Login Start*. In talking through the flow of this task, we realized that we would need to write a servlet that would blow away an existing cookie. This needs to happen when a user accesses our site from a computer that has a cookie belonging to someone else. The system welcomes users to the site by putting their e-mail address on a welcome page, along with a button users can click if that is not their e-mail address. If they click that button, we have to destroy the existing cookie and then let the user log in.

So we made a new task named *Reset Servlet* that blew away cookies. The subsequent history of this task is pretty interesting, and we'll discuss it further in the next few chapters. (See Task 6.9.)

Jim signed up for this new task and estimated its cost as four ideal hours. This is a good example of how the act of estimation may cause new tasks to be discovered.

Then we continued with our analysis of Task 6.1: *Login Start*. We had previous experience with servlets, so we knew what to expect. After considering the tests involved, Jim felt that this task would take four ideal hours.[1]

---

1. At this point it might seem that we were assuming that all servlets were going to take four hours.

Reset Servlet

A servlet that blows away a cookie and brings up the login page.

TASK 6.9 Reset Servlet Task

So far, all the estimates have been Jim's. That's because he's the one who signed up for these tasks. Bob has been helping, but the estimates belong to Jim.

Then we estimated Task 6.2: *Login Page HTML*. This task is all HTML. We talked for a bit about how to test it. We decided to dump the output of the HTML to SnoopServlet to verify that the fields were named and filled in correctly. Because this was all HTML, we didn't automate the test; we figured we'd run it manually. (This hurt us later.) Jim estimated this task as another four ideal hours.

Once again, the discussion about Task 6.3: *Login Task* focused on how to test the functionality, rather than on the functionality itself. After lengthy deliberations, Jim decided this would take about eight ideal hours.

Next it was Bob's turn to estimate. Seeing that Task 6.7: *Registration HTML*, was similar to Task 6.2: *Login Page HTML*, he decided to give it the same estimate of four ideal hours. It is usually a good idea to base an estimate on similar tasks. However, it is not usually a good idea to choose someone else's estimate as your own. Bob and Jim have worked together for a long time and knew they would be pairing on this. So Bob felt comfortable with the estimates.

Bob did the same thing for Task 6.8: *Registration Task Servlet*. He considered it to be similar to Task 6.3: *Login Task* and used the same estimate of eight ideal hours. This might have been risky, because *Registration Task Servlet* involved sending e-mail and Task 6.3: *Login Task* did not. However, during exploration, we did a spike on sending e-mail (see page 23). This showed that e-mail was fairly simple to do and gave Bob confidence in the estimate.

Estimation continued in this vein until all tasks were complete. The estimates can be seen in Table 6.2.

In the previous chapter, we had arbitrarily decided to set our velocity to 2.5. Thus, in a one-week iteration, two people can only do five days (40 hours) worth of tasks. Our estimates summed to 50 hours. Clearly we had a problem.

Our solution was less than optimal. We didn't want to go back to Lowell and tell him, once again, that he had to settle for less than we had promised. We also had no confidence in our chosen velocity. So we decided to "guts" it and let the iteration stand at 50 hours.

This was the wrong thing to do. What we should have done was go back to Lowell and ask him to remove stories from the plan until we had only 40 hours in the iteration. Then we could have built some trust with Lowell by being more up front with our planning process. Instead, we fell back on old habits.

Also, Lowell wasn't there. He was on the phone, and we didn't involve him in the final discussions about the iteration.

TABLE 6.2 Task Estimate Table for Iteration 1

Task	Programmer	Estimate (ideal hours)
Task 6.1: *Login Start*	Jim	4
Task 6.2: *Login Page HTML*	Jim	4
Task 6.3: *Login Task*	Jim	8
Task 6.4: *Enter as Guest Task*	Bob	4
Task 6.5: *Forgot Password Task*	Bob	6
Task 6.6: *Create Database Task*	Jim	8
Task 6.7: *Registration HTML*	Bob	4
Task 6.8: *Registration Task Servlet*	Bob	8
Task 6.9: *Reset Servlet Task*	Jim	4
Total		50

Later, Lowell found out about the discrepancy and was not pleased. He was upset that we had estimated the stories and set his expectation one way, and then a few hours later had estimated the tasks with a different result.

This is "the first iteration effect." Velocity is unknown or inconsistent, so estimates have huge error bars. Fortunately, this is only one iteration, one week, so the errors have a small total cost. Furthermore, as iteration follows iteration, the estimates will become more consistent and the velocity will be known. But none of these things made either Lowell or us feel any better about the first iteration plan.

Conclusion

We spent 90 minutes planning a one-week iteration. This is a ratio of nearly 27:1. By this metric a three-week iteration would take half a day to plan.

We were dismayed, but not surprised, to find that task estimates and story estimates are not automatically consistent. Our large-scale estimates of stories tended to be more optimistic than our small-scale estimates of tasks. One reason for this discrepancy may have been that we were not thinking about tests when we estimated the stories, but thought a lot about tests when estimating tasks. We expect the next iteration to be better.

Also, we made a mistake by letting Lowell escape from the last half of iteration planning. Had he been present and engaged, there would have been fewer surprises for him to deal with later.

Finally, we should not have agreed to do a 50-hour iteration. Of all the mistakes made, this was the worst.

Chapter 7

Beginning
the First Iteration

No battle plan ever survives contact with the enemy.
—One of Murphy's Military Laws

Plans Are One Thing, Reality Is Another

No sooner had we completed the iteration plan than our priorities underwent dramatic changes. What those changes were is not important. What is important is that the time we had budgeted to work on the project was sharply curtailed. In effect, we had less than one day per week to dedicate to the project. As a result the iteration took much longer in real time than we had planned.

Working one day per week on a project is not usually a good idea. After reading our experience, you can judge for yourself how good an idea it was in this case.

Development was done by four engineers working in pairs at different times and in different environments. Jim Newkirk was part of each pair. The other participants were James Grenning, Brian Button, and Bob Martin.

The computer we used was Jim's laptop. Pairing on a laptop is inconvenient at best. The screen is small, the viewing angles can be narrow, the keyboard is cramped, it's not easy to move the keyboard back and forth, and so on. But we managed.

Starting the Iteration

Which task should we start first? It seemed clear to us that all the tasks depended on the database. So we decided to implement Task 6.6: *Create Database Task* first.

Infrastructure

In hindsight, this might not have been the best approach. We were assuming that the other tasks needed the infrastructure of the database. Later in the project, we realized that tasks could be implemented and tested without the underlying infrastructure (see *Spoofing* on page 92). As you will see, the code for *Create Database Task* went through many changes as we implemented the other tasks. Our original assumptions about the infrastructure turned out to be naive. It seems likely that had we implemented the other tasks first, our understanding of their infrastructure needs would have prevented this thrashing.

First we set up the schema in the Microsoft Access database. We talked to Lowell about the size of the fields and other details. He told us that he really didn't need some of the fields that were specified on the task card (see Task 6.6: *Create Database Task*, on page 39). All we really needed were first name, last name, organization, e-mail address, password, and notification. We didn't need the address and phone number. So we built the database accordingly.

Next we created the appropriate ODBC binding, named website-users. Then we started writing a test module named DatabaseAccessTest that would test whether or not we could read and write customers. Before we got very far, however, we realized that we needed to test whether or not we could connect to the database. So we wrote Database-ConnectionTest. (See Listing 7.1.)

We used the popular JUnit[1] test framework to organize and execute our tests. We compiled and ran this test and the test passed, so we knew that we could connect to the database.

The connection code in Listing 7.1 is pretty ugly, and we didn't want to proliferate it. So we created a class named Database that would

---

1. Beck, K., and E. Gamma. 2001. "JUnit Open-Source Testing Framework." Available from http://www.junit.org.

LISTING 7.1 DatabaseConnectionTest—Version 1

```java
import junit.framework.*;
import java.sql.*;

public class DatabaseConnectionTest extends TestCase
{
  static
  {
    try
    {
      Class.forName( "sun.jdbc.odbc.JdbcOdbcDriver" );
    }
    catch(ClassNotFoundException e)
    {
      e.printStackTrace();
      System.exit(1);
    }
  }

  public DatabaseConnectionTest(String name)
  {
    super(name);
  }

  public static Test suite()
  {
    return new TestSuite(DatabaseConnectionTest.class);
  }

  public void testConnect() throws Throwable
  {
    Connection con = DriverManager.getConnection(
      "jdbc:odbc:websiteusers", "", "" );

    assert(!con.isClosed());
    con.close();
    assert(con.isClosed());
  }
}
```

encapsulate it. Again, we made the mistake of considering infrastructure early. We anticipated that the ugly code would proliferate, rather than waiting to see hints of that proliferation. In hindsight, it would have been better to wait. As you will see, the Database class thrashed quite a bit as the application grew. (See Listing 7.2.)

LISTING 7.2 Database—Version 1

```java
import java.sql.*;

public class Database
{
  static
  {
    try
    {
      Class.forName( "sun.jdbc.odbc.JdbcOdbcDriver" );
    }
    catch(ClassNotFoundException e)
    {
      e.printStackTrace();
      System.exit(1);
    }
  }

  public Database(String ds) throws ClassNotFoundException,
                                    SQLException
  {
    dataSource = ds;
  }

  public void open() throws SQLException
  {
    con = DriverManager.getConnection( "jdbc:odbc:" +
          dataSource, "", "" );
  }

  public boolean isOpen() throws SQLException
  {
    return !con.isClosed();
  }

  public void close() throws SQLException
  {
```

LISTING 7.2 Database—Version 1 (*continued*)

```
      con.close();
  }

  private Connection con;
  private String dataSource;
}
```

The Database object gave us a nice place to put the isOpen function. This function made more sense to us than the isClosed function in the Connection class.

Next we refactored DatabaseConnectionTest to use the Database object. This made it smaller and more readable. (See Listing 7.3.)

LISTING 7.3 DatabaseConnectionTest—Version 2

```
import junit.framework.*;
import java.sql.*;

public class DatabaseConnectionTest extends TestCase
{

  public DatabaseConnectionTest(String name)
  {
    super(name);
  }

  public static Test suite()
  {
    return new TestSuite(DatabaseConnectionTest.class);
  }

  public void testConnect() throws Throwable
  {
    Database db = new Database( "websiteusers" );
    db.open();

    assert(db.isOpen());
    db.close();
    assert(!db.isOpen());
  }
}
```

Next we started thinking about how to access the database. Our first test case described how we would read a `Customer` out of the database. To write this test case, we decided that we needed a `Customer` class to hold the data and a `findCustomerByEmail` method. (See Listing 7.4.)

LISTING 7.4 DatabaseAccessTest

```
import junit.framework.*;

public class DatabaseAccessTest extends TestCase
{
  private Database db;

  public DatabaseAccessTest(String name)
  {
    super(name);
  }

  protected void setUp() throws Exception
  {
    db = new Database("websiteusers");
    db.open();
  }

  protected void tearDown() throws Exception
  {
    db.close();
  }

  public static Test suite()
  {
    return new TestSuite(DatabaseAccessTest.class);
  }

  public void testRead() throws Exception
  {
    Customer c = db.findCustomerByEmail(
                    "newkirk@objectmentor.com");
    assert(c != null);

    assertEquals("newkirk@objectmentor.com",
                 c.getEmailAddress());
    assertEquals("jim", c.getPassword());
    assertEquals("James", c.getFirstName());
```

LISTING 7.4 DatabaseAccessTest (*continued*)

```
    assertEquals("Newkirk", c.getLastName());
    assertEquals("Object Mentor, Inc.",
                 c.getOrganization());
    assert(c.getNotification());
  }
}
```

Clearly, Listing 7.4 won't compile unless we create a Customer class. So, we wrote a new test class called CustomerTest. This test helped us figure out what data and methods should be in a Customer class. (See Listing 7.5.)

LISTING 7.5 CustomerTest

```
import junit.framework.*;

public class CustomerTest extends TestCase
{
  public CustomerTest(String name)
  {
    super(name);
  }

  public static Test suite()
  {
    return new TestSuite(CustomerTest.class);
  }

  public void testCreate()
  {
    Customer c = new Customer("newkirk@objectmentor.com",
      "password",
      "James",
      "Newkirk",
      "Object Mentor, Inc.",
      true);

    assertEquals("newkirk@objectmentor.com",
                 c.getEmailAddress());
    assertEquals("password", c.getPassword());
```

Listing continued on next page.

LISTING 7.5 CustomerTest *(continued)*

```
    assertEquals("James", c.getFirstName());
    assertEquals("Newkirk", c.getLastName());
    assertEquals("Object Mentor, Inc.",
              c.getOrganization());

    assert(c.getNotification());
  }
}
```

Now that we had the CustomerTest in place, we could write the Customer class itself. This class contained only data fields with appropriate accessors. (See Listing 7.6.)

LISTING 7.6 Customer

```
class Customer
{
  private String email;
  private String firstName;
  private String lastName;
  private String password;
  private boolean notification;
  private String organization;

  public Customer(String email,
                  String password,
                  String firstName,
                  String lastName,
                  String organization,
                  boolean notify)
  {
    this.email = email;
    this.password = password;
    this.firstName = firstName;
    this.lastName = lastName;
    this.notification = notify;
    this.organization = organization;
  }
```

LISTING 7.6 Customer *(continued)*

```
   public String getEmailAddress()
   {
     return email;
   }

   public String getFirstName()
   {
     return firstName;
   }

   public String getLastName()
   {
     return lastName;
   }

   public String getPassword()
   {
     return password;
   }

   public boolean getNotification()
   {
     return notification;
   }

   public String getOrganization()
   {
     return organization;
   }
}
```

Now the CustomerTest class compiled and the test passed, but DatabaseAccessTest still didn't compile because we didn't have findCustomerByEmail in the Database class. (See Listing 7.7.)

We manually added the newkirk@objectmentor.com Customer that would make the test in Listing 7.4 pass. But getting the code in Listing 7.7 to work was not without its difficulties. First, we forgot to put a password field into the database schema. This caused an ODBC error. Once we fixed the schema, the JVM started crashing every time we ran the program. We finally traced this to our failure to close the ResultSet. So we added the rs.close() line at the end of Listing 7.7. Eventually we got the tests to pass.

LISTING 7.7 Customer.findCustomerByEmail

```
public Customer findCustomerByEmail(String emailAddress)
                        throws SQLException
  {
    Statement statement = con.createStatement();

    ResultSet rs = statement.executeQuery(
        "SELECT * FROM userlist WHERE emailAddress = '" +
        emailAddress + "'");
    Customer c = null;
    boolean found = false;
    while(rs.next() && !found)
    {
      found = true;
      c = new Customer(rs.getString("emailAddress"),
                       rs.getString("password"),
                       rs.getString("firstName"),
                       rs.getString("lastName"),
                       rs.getString("organization"),
                       rs.getBoolean("notification"));
    }
    rs.close();

    return c;
  }
```

Our next test case was for adding a Customer. (See Listing 7.8.) The first thing we wanted to check was that invoking findCustomerByEmail on a known bad e-mail address would return null. So we wrote testNull.

Next, we wrote testAdd(). We made sure the Customer was not in the database, then we added it, and then we invoked findCustomerByEmail to fetch the Customer back. We checked to be sure the Customer we wrote was equal to the Customer we read.

After we wrote Database.addCustomer this compiled but failed our tests. After some thought, we realized that assertEquals uses the Java equals method. We had forgotten to override equals in Customer.

Instead of simply writing equals in Customer, we wrote the test case first. (See Listing 7.9.)

LISTING 7.8 DatabaseAccessTest.{testNull,testAdd}

```
public void testNull() throws Exception
{
  Customer c =
    db.findCustomerByEmail("noname@badvalue.com");
  assert(c == null);
}

public void testAdd() throws Exception
{
  String email = "123@universe.com";
  Customer c = new Customer(email,
    "456",
    "First",
    "Last",
    "The Universe",
    false);

  assert(db.findCustomerByEmail(email) == null);

  db.addCustomer(c);

  Customer dbCustomer = db.findCustomerByEmail(email);
  assert(dbCustomer != null);
  assertEquals(c, dbCustomer);
}
```

LISTING 7.9 CustomerTest.testEquals()

```
public void testEquals()
{
  Customer c1 = new Customer("button@objectmentor.com",
    "brian",
    "Brian",
    "Button",
    "Object Mentor, Inc.",
    false);

  Customer c2 = new Customer("newkirk@objectmentor.com",
    "password",
    "James",
    "Newkirk",
```

Listing continued on next page.

LISTING 7.9 `CustomerTest.testEquals()` (*continued*)

```
        "Object Mentor, Inc.",
        true);

    Customer c3 = new Customer("button@objectmentor.com",
        "brian",
        "Brian",
        "Button",
        "Object Mentor, Inc.",
        false);

    assert(!c1.equals(c2));
    assert(c1.equals(c3));
    assert(!c1.equals( null ));
    assert(!c1.equals( new String( "" )));
    assert( c1.equals( c1 ));
  }
```

Of course it fails, for the same reason that `testAdd` failed. The `equals` method of `Customer` had not yet been overridden. So, now that we had a failing test case that showed that `Customer.equals` did not work properly, we could make it pass. (See Listing 7.10.)

LISTING 7.10 `Customer.equals()`

```
public boolean equals(Object o)
{
    if( o == this ) return true;
    if( o == null ) return false;
    if( o instanceof Customer )
    {
      Customer rhs = ( Customer )o;
      return (
        (email.equals(rhs.getEmailAddress())) &&
        (password.equals(rhs.getPassword())) &&
        (organization.equals(rhs.getOrganization())) &&
        (firstName.equals(rhs.getFirstName())) &&
        (lastName.equals(rhs.getLastName())) &&
        (notification == rhs.getNotification())
      );
    }

    return false;
}
```

Once Listing 7.10 was compiled, `CustomerTest` passed. So we ran `DatabaseAccessTest`. It too passed.

Test Isolation

You might be wondering why we wrote `testEquals` in `CustomerTest`. Why didn't we just write `Customer.equals` and then run the `DatabaseAccessTest` to see if it went green?

Failure of `testAdd` implies that there is something wrong with `Database.addCustomer`. However, `Database.addCustomer` was working just fine. The problem was in `Customer.equals`. We wanted the flaw to be caught and reported in the right place.

Also, there might have been something wrong with `Database.addCustomer` that was being masked by the failure of `Customer.equals`. If the test had still failed, we would not have known whether the problem was in `Customer.equals`, in `Database.addCustomer`, or in `findCustomerByEmail`. We would probably have spent a lot of time debugging functions that were working. By creating `testEquals`, we isolated the problem.

Hit the Button Twice

With the tests having passed, we hit the test button again. This time the tests failed! Clearly, the system had changed state between the two test runs.

Sure enough, we forgot to remove the `Customer` in `testAdd`. The second time we ran it, the `Customer` was there. We needed to remove the `Customer` at the end of `testAdd`.

We wrote `Database.deleteCustomer()`, called it from the end of `testAdd`, and the test passes. (See Listing 7.11.)

LISTING 7.11 Database.deleteCustomer

```
public void deleteUser(String emailAddress)
                  throws SQLException
{
    Statement statement = con.createStatement( );
    statement.executeUpdate(
        "DELETE FROM userlist WHERE emailAddress = '" +
        emailAddress + "'" );
}
```

Oops

We forgot to write `testRemove`. Here we are, months later, writing this chapter, and we notice that we forgot an important test case. Disciplines are hard to maintain, especially when you are trying to learn them. An experienced coach might have helped us remember them better.

Finishing Up

Our last actions for this task were to change the name of the `Customer` class to `User`. We felt this was clearer. The people who use our Web site are not necessarily customers.

Finally we added all three test suites into a supersuite named `AllDatabaseTests`. We compiled and ran it, and the test passed. (See Listing 7.12.)

LISTING 7.12 `AllDatabaseTests`

```
import junit.framework.*;

public class AllDatabaseTests
{

  public static void main (String[] args)
  {
    junit.textui.TestRunner.run (suite());
  }

  public static Test suite ( )
  {
    TestSuite suite= new TestSuite("All Database Tests");
    suite.addTest(UserTest.suite());
    suite.addTest(DatabaseAccessTest.suite());
    suite.addTest(DatabaseConnectionTest.suite());
    return suite;
  }
}
```

Conclusion

The total time for this task was four hours. The estimate had been eight.

Even though we finished with half the expected effort, we still felt we were spending a lot of time writing and tweaking the test code. Perhaps this was because we were doing our design by writing the tests. Or perhaps we were just focusing on tests because writing tests first was new to us.

We made some mistakes in the development of this task. First, because we were new at test-first design, we forgot to write the test case for `removeCustomer`. More importantly, the decision to do this task first was based on our anticipation of the need for infrastructure. As you will see later, this code thrashes. We should have let the rest of the code tell us what kind of infrastructure it needed, rather than trying to dictate the infrastructure up front.

We also did some things right. We wrote lots of tests, we isolated tests such as `CustomerTest.testEquals`, we weren't afraid to change the name of the `Customer` class, and we ran our tests every time we made a change.

A big factor in our fearlessness to make changes was the existence of the tests. When we changed `Customer` to `User`, we touched every module we had written. Yet the tests showed us that we hadn't broken anything.

Tracking

Table 7.1 describes the tasks that have been completed with the actual values.

TABLE 7.1 Current Tracking Information

Task	Programmer	Estimate (ideal hours)	Actual hours
Task 6.1: *Login Start*	Jim	4	Not started
Task 6.2: *Login Page HTML*	Jim	4	Not started
Task 6.3: *Login Task*	Jim	8	Not started

Table continued on next page.

TABLE 7.1 Current Tracking Information (*continued*)

Task	Programmer	Estimate (ideal hours)	Actual hours
Task 6.4: *Enter as Guest Task*	Bob	4	Not started
Task 6.5: *Forgot Password Task*	Bob	6	Not started
Task 6.6: *Create Database Task*	Jim	8	4
Task 6.7: *Registration HTML*	Bob	4	Not started
Task 6.8: *Registration Task Servlet*	Bob	8	Not started
Task 6.9: *Reset Servlet Task*	Jim	4	Not started
Total		50	4

Chapter 8

Task 6.3: Login Task

Our next task was Task 6.3: *Login Task*. To implement this task, we needed a way to trigger the login process. Some of our pages are open to the public, and some are reserved for registered users. If users click on a link that takes them to a reserved page, and they are not logged in, we want to take them to the login page first. Once they have logged in successfully, we want to automatically take them to the page they requested.

Protected Pages

We conducted a spike to find a way to protect a page and determine whether a user had already logged in or not during the session. Clearly, we did not want to force the user to log in more than once per session.

The spike led us to create the `CheckForLogin` servlet. This servlet is included at the front of every protected page. It checks to see if the e-mail address of a logged in user has been stored in the current session. (See Listing 8.1.)

To protect a page the following line must appear at the top:

```
<servlet code=CheckForLogin></SERVLET>
```

This takes advantage of server side include and requires that the page be an `.shtml`.

LISTING 8.1 CheckForLogin

```
public class CheckForLogin extends HttpServlet
{
  public void service(HttpServletRequest request,
                      HttpServletResponse response)
    throws ServletException, IOException
  {
    HttpSession s = request.getSession(true);

    String name = (String)s.getValue("email");
    if(name == null || name.length() == 0)
        redirect(request, response);
  }

  private void redirect(HttpServletRequest request,
                        HttpServletResponse response)
  throws ServletException, IOException

  {
      response.sendRedirect(
        "/userproject/login.jsp?url=" +
        request.getRequestURI());
  }
}
```

This scheme was adequate for the purposes of our tests and for ful-
filling the user story, but was not the best long-term solution. In the
longer term, we'd want a much more flexible way to protect certain
pages without necessarily restricting them to being .shtml or .jsp.
However, we had no user stories to drive us to implement the more
flexible solution.

As it turned out, it was a good thing we didn't spend a lot of time
on the more flexible solution. By the conclusion of the first release,
Lowell had decided not to protect *any* pages and to simply allow users
to log in if they wanted to. It would have been a shame to delay the
first release for a mechanism that our customer wouldn't use.

The CheckForLogin servlet redirects either to the desired page or to
the login page, depending upon whether the user is already logged in
or not. The login.jsp file presents the login page to the user. We used a
very simple version of this page for our tests. (See Listing 8.2.)

LISTING 8.2 `login.jsp`

```
<HTML>
<Head>
<Title>XP In Practice Login Page</Title>
</Head>

<Body>
<div align="center">
<center>
<table border="1" cellspacing="1" cellpadding="4">
<tr>
<td>
<p align="center">Current Member</p>
<form method="POST"
action="/servlet/LoginServlet">
<p><input type="text" name="emailAddress"
size="30"> <b>email<br>
</b><input type="password" name="password"
size="30"> <b>password</b></p>
<p><input type="checkbox" name="remember"
value="ON"><b>Please remember </b></p>
<p><input type="submit" value="Login"
name="B1">
<input type="reset" value="Reset"
name="B2"></p>
<input type=hidden name="url"
value="<%= request.getParameter("url") %>">
</form>
</td>
</tr>
</table>
</center>
</div>
</Body>
</HTML>
```

We Didn't Write Tests

We couldn't figure out a convenient way to write automatic unit tests for Java Server Pages (JSP) and servlet modules. We thought these modules were fairly simple, so we decided that a suite of manual tests, conducted through the browser, would be sufficient. Listing 8.3 is an example of these manual tests.

LISTING 8.3 Manual Login Test

---

1. Kill the current browser (had to do this to remove the current session; JSP creates sessions for you, so even though we thought we did not create one, we had one anyway).

2. Go to the home page http://127.0.0.1/userproject/default.html.

3. Click on the Protected Page link.

4. The login page should be brought up.

5. Enter user information and hit Login.

6. You should be sent to a page that says "Protected Page."

7. Repeat step 2.

8. Repeat step 3.

9. You should be sent to a page that says "Protected Page."

However, this was not a good choice. We eventually did a lot of refactoring of all this "simple" code. Tests would have been a big help. Also, these tests took a lot of time to run and, being manual, were error prone. So, we should have spent the time to invent a fixture for testing the servlets and JSPs.

Logging In

The login.jsp page collected the necessary data from the user and then invoked LoginServlet. This servlet's job was to ascertain whether the user existed in the database and whether or not the password provided by login.jsp matched the one in the database. How was LoginServlet going to do this?

Rather than just writing LoginServlet on the fly, we decided to write a test that demonstrated that a valid user could be logged in. So we wrote DatabaseAccessTest.testLogin(). (See Listing 8.4.)

In the process of writing this test, we decided that password comparison was the jurisdiction of the User object and should not be conducted by some other entity. So we wrote User.validate. (See Listing 8.5.)

- -

LISTING 8.4 DatabaseAccessTest.testLogin

```
public void testLogin() throws Exception
{
  User u = db.findUserByEmail("bbutton@objectmentor.com");
  assert(u.validate("brian"));
}
```

LISTING 8.5 User.validate

```
public boolean validate(String password)
{
  return (this.password.equals(password));
}
```

This made the tests pass. Then we were ready to write LoginServlet. (See Listing 8.6.)

It is interesting to note that there is a strong similarity between DatabaseAccessTest.testLogin() and LoginServlet. This is a pattern that we will see many other times. The reason is simply that the tests simulate actual clients, and servlets are clients.

As we wrote the LoginServlet, we thought of some more test cases. What would happen if we passed a null, or a zero-length String, into findUserByEmail? So, we wrote these new test cases and ran them. (See Listing 8.7.)

We renamed the existing testNull to testNotFound, and then implemented the new testNull and testZeroLengthEmail. These all passed without modifying the existing code.

Even though we did not uncover any bugs by writing these tests, we don't consider the effort wasted. We now know that future changes to the code cannot break the system if they pass nulls or zero length strings.

Closing Unopened Databases

Careful inspection of LoginServlet will show that the close method of Database can be called, even though the creation of the Database instance failed. Is this a problem? Probably.

LISTING 8.6 LoginServlet

```
public class LoginServlet extends HttpServlet
{
  public void service(HttpServletRequest request,
                      HttpServletResponse response)
  throws ServletException, IOException
  {
    HttpSession s = request.getSession(true);

    String email = request.getParameter("emailAddress");
    String password = request.getParameter("password");

    Database db = null;
    try
    {
      db = new Database("websiteusers");
      db.open();

      User u = db.findUserByEmail(email);
      if( u != null)
      {
        if (u.validate(password))
        {
          s.putValue("email", email);
        }
      }
    }
    catch(SQLException e)
    {}
    finally
    {
      try
      { db.close();}
      catch(SQLException e)
      {}
    }

    redirect(request, response);
  }

  private void redirect(HttpServletRequest request,
                        HttpServletResponse response)
    throws ServletException, IOException
```

LISTING 8.6 LoginServlet (*continued*)

```
    {
      String url = (String)request.getParameter("url");
      if(url == null)
        url = "http://croup/userproject";
      response.sendRedirect(url);
    }
  }
```

LISTING 8.7 DatabaseAccessTest.{testNotFound, testNull, testZeroLengthEmail}

```
  public void testNotFound() throws Exception
  {
      User u = db.findUserByEmail("noname@badvalue.com");
      assert(u == null);
  }

  public void testNull() throws Exception
  {
      User u = db.findUserByEmail(null);
      assert(u == null);
  }

  public void testZeroLengthEmail() throws Exception
  {
      User u = db.findUserByEmail("");
      assert(u == null);
  }
```

To prove whether this was problematic, we wrote a test case that called close on an unopened Database instance. Sure enough, it crashed the JVM. So we changed LoginServlet to protect against this.

This was the first hint that things were not right with the structure of the Database class. The infrastructure we created by anticipation was already showing some chinks. More would appear.

Test Aware

As our experience with tests increased, we found ourselves depending on them more and more. We wanted feedback on everything we did.

This trend has continued to this day to the extent that now test cases are the very first things we consider.

Cookies

As shown in User Story 4.9: *Transparent Login,* on page 22, Lowell wanted frequent users to be freed from the need to log in every session. The usual way to allow this is for the system to write cookies into the users' browsers.

The writing of cookies is controlled by the servlets, but it also involves the client browser and the Web server. We felt that automatically testing this would be even more difficult than testing servlets. This was an extension of our justification not to *automatically* test servlets. (See page 65.) However, that initial justification was based on servlets being simple. The servlets were not so simple anymore. (See Listing 8.8.)

To make matters worse, the manual test we were using to test the login servlet had to grow quite a bit to support cookies. (See Listing 8.9.) So it was becoming more and more difficult to run the test.

Our decision not to test servlets was coming back to haunt us. It would haunt us more as time went by.

We felt LoginServlet was getting too long. It was time to refactor it. Using the Extract Method[1] refactoring, we pulled all the database access code into a function named validateLogin. The result was much simpler. (See 8.10.)

The validateLogin method does not depend upon the servlet environment. There is no need for it to be in LoginServlet. Indeed, it is better suited as a method of Database. By moving it, we make LoginServlet independent of JDBC and classes such as SQLException. This is nice.

In preparation to move the validateLogin method, we wrote DatabaseAccessTest.testValidateLogin. (See Listing 8.11.)

Finally, using the Move Method[2] refactoring, we relocated validateLogin into the Database class.

---

1. Fowler, M. 1999. *Refactoring: Improving the design of existing code.* Reading, MA, Addison-Wesley.
2. Ibid.

LISTING 8.8 LoginServlet after Cookies

```java
public class LoginServlet extends HttpServlet
{
  public void service(HttpServletRequest request,
                      HttpServletResponse response)
    throws ServletException, IOException
  {
    HttpSession s = request.getSession(true);

    String email = request.getParameter("emailAddress");
    String password = request.getParameter("password");

    boolean remember = true;
    String stringRem = request.getParameter("remember");
    if(stringRem == null)
      remember = false;

    Database db = null;
    try
    {
      db = new Database("websiteusers");
      db.open();

      User u = db.findUserByEmail(email);
      if( u != null)
      {
        if (u.validate(password))
        {
          s.putValue("email", email);
          if ( remember )
          {
            final int oneYear = 86400*365;
            Cookie cookie = new Cookie("email", email);
            cookie.setMaxAge(oneYear);
            cookie.setPath("/userproject");
            response.addCookie(cookie);
          }
        }
      }
    }
    catch(SQLException e)
    {}
    finally
```

Listing continued on next page.

LISTING 8.8 LoginServlet after Cookies (*continued*)

```
    {
      try
      { if(db != null) db.close();}
      catch(SQLException e)
      {}
    }

    redirect(request, response);
  }
```

LISTING 8.9 Manual Test for Login with Cookies

1. Kill the current browser. (Had to do this to remove the current session. JSP creates sessions for you, so even though we thought we did not create one, we had one anyway.)
2. Set browser settings to indicate prompt for acceptance of cookies.
3. Go to the home page http://127.0.0.1/userproject/default.html.
4. Click on the Protected Page link.
5. A dialog should pop up, indicating that a session cookie is being placed. Click OK.
6. The login page should be brought up.
7. Enter user information and hit login; remember to select the remember checkbox.
8. You should be sent to a page that says "Protected Page."
9. A dialog will pop up, indicating another cookie is being placed. This one is the permanent one. It should have a date about one year in the future.
10. Repeat step 3.
11. Repeat step 4.
12. You should be sent to a page that says "Protected Page."
13. Kill the current browser.
14. Repeat step 3.
15. Repeat step 4.
16. You should be taken to the protected page.

LISTING 8.10 LoginServlet refactored

```java
public class LoginServlet extends HttpServlet
{
  public void service(HttpServletRequest request,
                       HttpServletResponse response)
    throws ServletException, IOException
  {
    HttpSession s = request.getSession(true);

    String email = request.getParameter("emailAddress");
    String password = request.getParameter("password");

    boolean remember = true;
    String stringRem = request.getParameter("remember");
    if(stringRem == null)
      remember = false;

    if (validateLogin(email, password))
    {
      s.putValue("email", email);
      if ( remember )
      {
        final int oneYear = 86400 * 365;
        Cookie cookie = new Cookie("email", email);
        cookie.setMaxAge(oneYear);
        cookie.setPath("/userproject");
        response.addCookie(cookie);
      }
    }

    redirect(request, response);
  }

  private boolean validateLogin(String email,
                                String password)
  {
    boolean result = false;

    Database db = null;
    try
    {
      db = new Database("websiteusers");
      db.open();
```

Listing continued on next page.

LISTING 8.10 LoginServlet refactored   (*continued*)

```
        User u = db.findUserByEmail(email);
        if( u != null)
        {
            result = u.validate(password);

        }
    }
    catch(SQLException e)
    {}
    finally
    {
        try
        { if(db != null) db.close();}
        catch(SQLException e)
        {}

    }
    return result;
}

private void redirect(HttpServletRequest request,
                      HttpServletResponse response)
    throws ServletException, IOException

{
    String url = (String)request.getParameter("url");
    if(url == null)
        url = "http://croup/userproject";
    response.sendRedirect(url);
}
}
```

LISTING 8.11 DatabaseAccessTest.testValidateLogin

```
public void testValidateLogin() throws Exception
{
    assert(Database.validateLogin(
                "newkirk@objectmentor.com", "jim"));
    assert(!Database.validateLogin(
                "123@objectmentor.com", "test"));
    assert(!Database.validateLogin("", "test"));
    assert(!Database.validateLogin(
                "newkirk@objectmentor.com", "test"));
    assert(!Database.validateLogin(null, null));
}
```

Login Task Conclusion

This task was estimated at eight hours. Implementation required eight hours. Nice.

Although we weren't quite aware of it yet, the failure to automatically test servlets was the biggest mistake we made in implementing this task.

For two reasons, the refactoring of the `LoginServlet`, simple as it was, was very satisfying. First, it was an improvement of the structure of the code. Second, we were able to move `validateLogin` from an untested servlet to a tested class.

Tracking

Table 8.1 describes the tasks that have been completed with the actual values.

TABLE 8.1 Current Tracking Information

Task	Programmer	Estimate (ideal hours)	Actual hours
Task 6.1: *Login Start*	Jim	4	Not started
Task 6.2: *Login Page HTML*	Jim	4	Not started
Task 6.3: *Login Task*	Jim	8	8
Task 6.4: *Enter as Guest Task*	Bob	4	Not started
Task 6.5: *Forgot Password Task*	Bob	6	Not started
Task 6.6: *Create Database Task*	Jim	8	4
Task 6.7: *Registration HTML*	Bob	4	Not started
Task 6.8: *Registration Task Servlet*	Bob	8	Not started
Task 6.9: *Reset Servlet Task*	Jim	4	Not started
Total		50	12

Chapter 9

A Flurry of Refactoring

An interesting chain of refactorings took place during the implementation of Task 6.4: *Enter as Guest Task*. This task allowed a user who did not want to log in to gain access to our site by logging in as a "guest." Guests have full access to the site for the current session.

A user could log in as a guest by pressing the "Login as Guest" button on the login page. This would execute the GuestServlet. (See Listing 9.1.)

This class worked fine. However, compare it with the current LoginServlet in Listing 9.2. Notice that there is a considerable amount of duplicated code. The redirect function and the doPost functions are identical, and there are other areas of the modules that show similarities.

Duplication of code is not allowed in XP. This is a rule named "Once and only once." When you see code duplication, it is your job to remove it. The mechanism we employed to remove this duplication was to create a new base class named FrontEndServlet (a terrible name that we rectified later). Both GuestServlet and LoginServlet were changed to inherit from this base. Then we moved the redirect function and the doPost function to the base class. This is the Pull up Method[1] refactoring. (See Listing 9.2.)

---

1. Fowler, M. 1999. *Refactoring: Improving the design of existing code.* Reading, MA, Addison-Wesley.

LISTING 9.1 GuestServlet—Refactoring 0

```
public class GuestServlet extends HttpServlet
{
  public void doPost(HttpServletRequest request,
                     HttpServletResponse response)
    throws ServletException, IOException
  {
    doGet(request, response);
  }

  public void doGet(HttpServletRequest request,
                    HttpServletResponse response)
    throws ServletException, IOException
  {
    HttpSession s = request.getSession(true);
    s.putValue("email", "guest");
    redirect(request, response);
  }

  private void redirect(HttpServletRequest request,
                        HttpServletResponse response)
    throws ServletException, IOException

  {
    String url = (String)request.getParameter("url");
    if(url == null)
      url = "http://croup/userproject";
    response.sendRedirect(url);
  }
}
```

The doGet methods of both LoginServlet and GuestServlet use the same protocol. They first perform their specific jobs, and then they redirect to the page referenced in the url parameter of the HttpServletRequest. FrontEndServlet, as seen in Listing 9.3, uses the Template Method[2] pattern to implement this protocol in one place and remove the duplication. The two servlets then implement the abstract execute function to provide their specific functionality. (See Listings 9.4 and 9.5.)

---

2. Gamma, E., R. Helm, R. Johnson, and J. Vlissides. 1995. *Design patterns: Elements of reusable object-oriented software*. Reading, MA: Addison-Wesley.

LISTING 9.2 LoginServlet—Refactoring 0

```java
public class LoginServlet extends HttpServlet
{
  public void doPost(HttpServletRequest request,
                     HttpServletResponse response)
    throws ServletException, IOException
  {
    doGet(request, response);
  }

  public void doGet(HttpServletRequest request,
                    HttpServletResponse response)
    throws ServletException, IOException
  {
    HttpSession s = request.getSession(true);

    String email = request.getParameter("emailAddress");
    String password = request.getParameter("password");

    boolean remember = true;
    String stringRem = request.getParameter("remember");
    if(stringRem == null)
      remember = false;

    if (Database.validateLogin(email, password))
    {
      s.putValue("email", email);
      if ( remember )
      {
        final int oneYear = 86400 * 365;
        Cookie cookie = new Cookie("email", email);
        cookie.setMaxAge(oneYear);
        cookie.setPath("/userproject");
        response.addCookie(cookie);
      }
    }
    redirect(request, response);
  }

  private void redirect(HttpServletRequest request,
                        HttpServletResponse response)
    throws ServletException, IOException
```

Listing continued on next page.

LISTING 9.2 LoginServlet—Refactoring 0 (*continued*)

```
  {
    String url = (String)request.getParameter("url");
    if(url == null)
      url = "http://croup/userproject";
    response.sendRedirect(url);
  }
}
```

LISTING 9.3 FrontEndServlet—Refactoring 1

```
public abstract class FrontEndServlet extends HttpServlet
{
  public abstract void execute(
          HttpServletRequest request,
          HttpServletResponse response)
    throws ServletException, IOException;

  public void doPost(HttpServletRequest request,
                     HttpServletResponse response)
     throws ServletException, IOException
  {
    doGet(request, response);
  }

  public void doGet(HttpServletRequest request,
                    HttpServletResponse response)
    throws ServletException, IOException
  {
    execute(request, response);
    redirect(request, response);
  }

  private void redirect(HttpServletRequest request,
                        HttpServletResponse response)
    throws ServletException, IOException
  {
    String url = (String)request.getParameter("url");
    if(url == null)
      url = "http://croup/userproject";
    response.sendRedirect(url);
  }
}
```

LISTING 9.4 GuestServlet—Refactoring 1

```java
public class GuestServlet extends FrontEndServlet
{
  public void execute(HttpServletRequest request,
                      HttpServletResponse response)
    throws ServletException, IOException
  {
    HttpSession s = request.getSession(true);
    s.putValue("email", "guest");
  }
}
```

LISTING 9.5 LoginServlet—Refactoring 1

```java
public class LoginServlet extends FrontEndServlet
{
  public void execute(HttpServletRequest request,
                      HttpServletResponse response)
    throws ServletException, IOException
  {
    HttpSession s = request.getSession(true);

    String email = request.getParameter("emailAddress");
    String password = request.getParameter("password");

    boolean remember = true;
    String stringRem = request.getParameter("remember");
    if(stringRem == null)
      remember = false;

    if (Database.validateLogin(email, password))
    {
      s.putValue("email", email);
      if ( remember )
      {
        final int oneYear = 86400 * 365;
        Cookie cookie = new Cookie("email", email);
        cookie.setMaxAge(oneYear);
        cookie.setPath("/userproject");
        response.addCookie(cookie);
      }
    }
  }
}
```

This refactoring had a dramatic effect on the code. GuestServlet is now quite small and easy to understand. LoginServlet is much better, but is still fairly long and busy. It does not "speak" about what it does, and it's hard to read and understand. But there are ways to improve this situation.

Refactoring LoginServlet

One powerful method of improving the readability of a method is to extract smaller methods and give them compelling names. (See Listing 9.6.)

LISTING 9.6 LoginServlet—Refactoring 2

```
public class LoginServlet extends FrontEndServlet
{
  HttpServletRequest itsRequest;
  HttpServletResponse itsResponse;
  HttpSession itsSession;
  String itsUserId;

  public void execute(HttpServletRequest request,
                      HttpServletResponse response)
    throws ServletException, IOException
  {
    itsRequest = request;
    itsResponse = response;
    itsSession = itsRequest.getSession(true);
    itsUserId = request.getParameter("emailAddress");

    String password = request.getParameter("password");
    if (Database.validateLogin(itsUserId, password))
    {
      saveUserInSession();
      if (shouldWriteCookie())
      {
        saveUserInCookie();
      }
    }
  }

  private boolean shouldWriteCookie()
  {
    boolean writeCookie = true;
    String stringRem = itsRequest.getParameter("remember");
```

LISTING 9.6 LoginServlet—Refactoring 2 (*continued*)

```
      if(stringRem == null)
        writeCookie = false;
      return writeCookie;
    }

    private void saveUserInSession()
    {
      itsSession.putValue("email", itsUserId);
    }

    private void saveUserInCookie()
    {
      final int oneYear = 86400 * 365;
      Cookie cookie = new Cookie("email", itsUserId);
      cookie.setMaxAge(oneYear);
      cookie.setPath("/userproject");
      itsResponse.addCookie(cookie);
    }
}
```

Listing 9.6 shows the result of a series of Extract Method refactorings. We did them in the following order: saveUserInCookie, saveUserInSession, and shouldWriteCookie. Initially, these functions had parameters such as request, response, e-mail, and so on. These parameters cluttered the code. So we changed all the parameters to instance variables, using the Change Parameter to Field[3] refactoring. The result is that the execute method of LoginServlet reads very nicely. It is still long, but much better than before.

The saveUserInSession function of LoginServlet is similar in purpose to the line in GuestServlet that stores the "guest" identification in the session. Thus both servlets have the need to store a user in the session. Using the Pull up Method refactoring, we moved saveUserInSession to FrontEndServlet and then called it from GuestServlet and LoginServlet.

Another commonality between the two servlets is the need for request, response, and session variables. So the fetching and storing of these variables was moved to the base class. (See Listing 9.7.)

---

3. See http://www.refactoring.com.

LISTING 9.7 FrontEndServlet—Refactoring 3

```java
public abstract class FrontEndServlet extends HttpServlet
{
  HttpServletRequest itsRequest;
  HttpServletResponse itsResponse;
  HttpSession itsSession;

  public abstract void execute()
    throws ServletException, IOException;

  public void doPost(HttpServletRequest request,
                     HttpServletResponse response)
      throws ServletException, IOException
  {
    doGet(request, response);
  }

  public void doGet(HttpServletRequest request,
                    HttpServletResponse response)
    throws ServletException, IOException
  {
    itsRequest = request;
    itsResponse = response;
    itsSession = itsRequest.getSession(true);

    execute();
    redirect();
  }

  protected void saveUserInSession(String userId)
  {
    itsSession.putValue("email", userId);
  }

  private void redirect()
    throws ServletException, IOException
  {
    String url = (String)itsRequest.getParameter("url");
    if(url == null)
      url = "http://croup/userproject";
    itsResponse.sendRedirect(url);
  }
}
```

The name `FrontEndServlet` is pretty hideous. After all this refactoring, we decided to change it to `RedirectingServlet`. This reflects the protocol encapsulated by the `TemplateMethod` pattern. The final result is shown in Listings 9.8 through 9.11.

LISTING 9.8 `RedirectingServlet`—Refactoring 4

```
public abstract class RedirectingServlet extends HttpServlet
{
  HttpServletRequest itsRequest;
  HttpServletResponse itsResponse;
  HttpSession itsSession;

  public abstract void execute()
    throws ServletException, IOException;

  public void doPost(HttpServletRequest request,
                     HttpServletResponse response)
    throws ServletException, IOException
  {
    doGet(request, response);
  }

  public void doGet(HttpServletRequest request,
                    HttpServletResponse response)
    throws ServletException, IOException
  {
    itsRequest = request;
    itsResponse = response;
    itsSession = itsRequest.getSession(true);

    execute();
    redirect();
  }

  protected void saveUserInSession(String userId)
  {
    itsSession.putValue("email", userId);
  }

  private void redirect()
    throws ServletException, IOException
```

Listing continued on next page.

LISTING 9.8 `RedirectingServlet`—Refactoring 4 *(continued)*

```
    {
      String url = (String)itsRequest.getParameter("url");
      if(url == null)
        url = "http://croup/userproject";
      itsResponse.sendRedirect(url);
    }
  }
```

LISTING 9.9 `LoginServlet`—Refactoring 4

```
public class LoginServlet extends RedirectingServlet
{
  String itsUserId;

  public void execute()
    throws ServletException, IOException
  {
    itsUserId = itsRequest.getParameter("emailAddress");

    String password = itsRequest.getParameter("password");
    if (Database.validateLogin(itsUserId, password))
    {
      saveUserInSession(itsUserId);
      if (shouldWriteCookie())
      {
        saveUserInCookie();
      }
    }
  }

  private boolean shouldWriteCookie()
  {
    boolean writeCookie = true;
    String stringRem = itsRequest.getParameter("remember");
    if(stringRem == null)
      writeCookie = false;
    return writeCookie;
  }

  private void saveUserInCookie()
  {
    final int oneYear = 86400 * 365;
    Cookie cookie = new Cookie("email", itsUserId);
```

LISTING 9.9 LoginServlet—Refactoring 4 (*continued*)

```
        cookie.setMaxAge(oneYear);
        cookie.setPath("/userproject");
        itsResponse.addCookie(cookie);
    }
}
```

LISTING 9.10 GuestServlet—Refactoring 4

```
public class GuestServlet extends RedirectingServlet
{
  public void execute()
      throws ServletException, IOException
  {
    saveUserInSession("guest");
  }
}
```

This is much better. These two servlets have become much easier to understand and maintain. And the amount of duplicated code has been dramatically reduced.

Conclusions

Second Instance Pays for Generality

Notice that we had no inkling of these refactorings until we wrote Guest-Servlet. Once GuestServlet appeared, however, the duplication between them was obvious, as were the abstractions necessary to eliminate it. It is not likely that we would have come up with RedirectingServlet in an up-front design. The motivations for creating it were based in the details of the code. This is an example of how designs evolve over time.

Was This Worth it?

A program has two values: There is the value that its users derive from its function, and there is the value inherent in its structure. If this second value is ignored, then the software becomes hard to read and hard to maintain. Over time it may have to be redesigned or just thrown away.

Most developers focus strongly on the value of function. This is a shame because the structure of the code is just as important. It is that structure that will give the code a long healthy life and protect the investment made by the customer.

Refactoring Without Automatic Tests Is Painful

This task took 1.5 hours to complete. A large part of this was the manual testing we had forced ourselves to use (see page 65). If we had automatic tests, these refactorings would have been much easier. We also would have done them in smaller steps. But because the overhead of testing was so high, we were driven to make larger changes before testing.

Would More Up-front Design Have Reduced the Refactoring?

Our experience has been that up-front design is not particularly good at predicting the eventual structure of the code. We see many systems that have been designed up front that badly need a lot of refactoring. So, up-front design would probably not have eliminated all the refactoring we did.

But a more important point should be made. Why should we want to prevent the refactoring? Is it somehow inefficient or unprofessional? We don't think so. We think refactoring is something that all software needs, whether it is designed up front or not. Reducing refactoring is not a realistic, nor even a desirable, goal.

Tracking

Table 9.1 describes the tasks that have been completed with the actual values.

TABLE 9.1 Current Tracking Information

Task	Programmer	Estimate (ideal hours)	Actual hours
Task 6.1: *Login Start*	Jim	4	Not started
Task 6.2: *Login Page HTML*	Jim	4	Not started
Task 6.3: *Login Task*	Jim	8	8
Task 6.4: *Enter as Guest Task*	Bob	4	1.5
Task 6.5: *Forgot Password Task*	Bob	6	Not started
Task 6.6: *Create Database Task*	Jim	8	4
Task 6.7: *Registration HTML*	Bob	4	Not started
Task 6.8: *Registration Task Servlet*	Bob	8	Not started
Task 6.9: *Reset Servlet Task*	Jim	4	Not started
Total		50	13.5

Chapter 10

sdrawkcaB gnikroW

Our next task was Task 6.5: *Forgot Password Task*. In this task, we needed to respond to a user who had forgotten his or her password. The idea was to put up a simple page that prompted the user for his or her e-mail address. This page would invoke a servlet that looked up the user's password and e-mailed it to him or her.

We still had not solved the problem of testing code in servlets. But we had learned from our past errors that servlets don't stay simple for long and need unit tests. Therefore we decided to put the bulk of the implementation in a testable, nonservlet class that would be called by the servlet.

TestNoUser

In thinking about the test cases, we realized that the most interesting ones were those in which we were trying to recover from either a database or mailer problem; for example, the user's e-mail address doesn't exist or the user's e-mail address confuses the mailer.

In previous tasks, we had loaded the database with special test entries. This forced us to go to extra effort to maintain these entries. Tests could give false results if the database entries were not properly managed (see *Hit the Button Twice* on page 59).

It would be better if we could completely control the test data and conditions from within the test case. We wondered how we could do this.

Ward Cunningham recommends writing the code you want to see, without worrying about the infrastructure that supports it. What did we want the tests to look like? Consider the test case in which the user enters an e-mail address that is not present in the database. We wrote the following:

```
assert(remind("nobody@home")==NOEMAILFOUND);
```

Based on this assertion, it was clear to us that the `remind` function's responsibilities were to look up the e-mail address in the database and then send the user the reminder message.

However, this particular test could be thwarted if someone accidentally put `nobody@home` into the database. We needed a way to isolate the test case from the database.

Spoofing

Rather than allowing `PasswordReminder` direct access to the database, we created an interface that `PasswordReminder` could use to access the database. Then, inside the test program, we created an anonymous inner class that implemented that interface and always returned `null`. (See Listings 10.1 and 10.2.)

This technique is called *spoofing*. We fooled the `PasswordReminder` into thinking it had a real database, when in reality we completely replaced the database with a *mock-object* that provided the behavior that we wanted to test.

This wasn't compiling yet, because we hadn't written `PasswordReminder`. But we were getting a good picture of what `PasswordReminder` should look like. So we wrote it. (See Listing 10.3.)

LISTING 10.1 PasswordReminderDatabase

```
public interface PasswordReminderDatabase
{
  public String findPasswordFromEmail(String email);
}
```

LISTING 10.2 ForgotPasswordTest.testNoUser—Refactoring 1

```
public void testNoUser()
{
    String noUser = "nobody@home";
    PasswordReminderDatabase db =
      new PasswordReminderDatabase()
    {
      public String findPasswordFromEmail(String email)
      {
        return null;
      }
    };
    PasswordReminder pr = new PasswordReminder(db);
    assert(pr.remind(noUser)==
        PasswordReminder.NOEMAILFOUND);
} // testNoUser
```

LISTING 10.3 PasswordReminder—Refactoring 1

```
public class PasswordReminder
{
  public static final int OK = 0;
  public static final int NOEMAILFOUND = 1;

  private PasswordReminderDatabase itsDb;
  public PasswordReminder(PasswordReminderDatabase db)
  {
    itsDb = db;
  }

  public int remind(String email)
  {
    int status;
    String password = itsDb.findPasswordFromEmail(email);
    if (password != null)
      status = OK;
    else
      status = NOEMAILFOUND;

    return status;
  }

}
```

Clearly, the function in Listing 10.3 is incomplete. It doesn't send the reminder e-mail message if the database access succeeds. But one step at a time. Right now our tests are passing.

Working Backwards

Notice the order in which we did this. We started with the initial assertion. We built the test case around that assertion, which helped us design the `PasswordReminder`. Then, finally, we wrote the incomplete version of `PasswordReminder`. We *backed* into the solution, starting from an initial assertion and a set of initial constraints. This kept us from guessing about anything. Instead of anticipating and inventing the infrastructure we needed, the methods we needed, or the objects we needed, we waited until the need was obvious.

But We Weren't Done

We may not have been done with `PasswordReminder`, but we were done with the current test case. We weren't going to write any more code into `PasswordReminder` until we had a failing test case.

TestGoodEmail

Next we wrote the test case that demonstrated that we could send the reminder message. We wanted that test case to look something like this:

```
assertEquals(PasswordReminder.OK,
             pr.remind("Bob"));
assertEquals("Bob", theToAddr);
assertEquals("Your Object Mentor Password",
             theSubj);
assertEquals(
  "Your Object Mentor Password is saba",
  theBody);
```

For the purposes of this test, we could assume that an OK return indicated that the mail was successfully sent. The rest of the asserts simply inspected the message to make sure it was properly formed.

We didn't want `PasswordReminder` to pass the e-mail message back to its caller. First, no one other than the test was interested in that message. Second, to deal with the message, the servlet would have to contain more code. And we didn't want to put code in places that were hard to test.

Also, this unit test was not intended to test that mail actually got sent. Rather its intent was to ensure that `PasswordReminder` had the correct logic. It would have been unnecessary to have e-mail sent every time we ran this test.

Both problems can be solved by spoofing the mailer. We created a `Mailer` interface, passed it into the `PasswordReminder`, and implemented the test case as shown in Listings 10.4 and 10.5.

LISTING 10.4 `Mailer`—Refactoring 1

```
public interface Mailer
{
  public void send(String to, String subj, String body);
}
```

LISTING 10.5 `ForgotPasswordTest`—Refactoring 2

```
public class ForgotPasswordTest extends TestCase
{

  private String theToAddr = "";
  private String theSubj = "";
  private String theBody = "";

  public void setup()
  {
    theToAddr = "";
    theSubj = "";
    theBody = "";
  }
  public void testGoodEmail()
  {
    PasswordReminderDatabase db =
      new PasswordReminderDatabase()
```

Listing continued on next page.

LISTING 10.5 ForgotPasswordTest—Refactoring 2 (*continued*)

```
   {
     public String findPasswordFromEmail(String email)
     {return "saba";}
   };

   Mailer m = new Mailer()
   {
     public boolean send(String to, String subj,
                         String body)
     {
       theToAddr = to;
       theSubj = subj;
       theBody = body;
     }
   };

   PasswordReminder pr = new PasswordReminder(db, m);
   assertEquals(PasswordReminder.OK, pr.remind("Bob"));
   assertEquals("Bob", theToAddr);
   assertEquals("Your Object Mentor Password", theSubj);
   assertEquals("Your Object Mentor Password is saba",
                theBody);
  }
}
```

Notice that the mock-mailer loads the instance variables of the test case with the data from the message. This allows the test case to later assert that their values are correct. All that this really tests is that PasswordReminder.remind actually calls Mailer.send with the right arguments.

Next we added the Mailer argument to PasswordReminder.remind, which would make this test case compile. The test failed, as expected.

Next we added the code to PasswordReminder.remind, which made the test pass. (See Listing 10.6.)

LISTING 10.6 PasswordReminder—Refactoring 2

```
public class PasswordReminder
{
  public static final int OK = 0;
  public static final int NOEMAILFOUND = 1;
```

LISTING 10.6 PasswordReminder—Refactoring 2   (*continued*)

```
    private PasswordReminderDatabase itsDb;
    private Mailer itsMailer;
    public PasswordReminder(PasswordReminderDatabase db,
                            Mailer m)
    {
      itsDb = db;
      itsMailer = m;
    }

    public int remind(String email)
    {
      int status = OK;
      String password = itsDb.findPasswordFromEmail(email);
      if (password != null)
      {
        itsMailer.send(
          email,
          "Your Object Mentor Password",
          "Your Object Mentor Password is " + password);
      }
      else
        status = NOEMAILFOUND;

      return status;
    }
  }
```

TestBadEmail

Our last test case involved a failure of the mailer to deal with an e-mail address. Once again we started with an assertion, as follows:

```
assertEquals(PasswordReminder.EMAILERROR,
             pr.remind("Bob"));
```

Next we changed Mailer.send to return a boolean and spoofed it to return false in this test case. Finally we added EMAILERROR to Password-Reminder.

The tests failed.

Next we changed PasswordReminder.remind to deal with the boolean return value from Mailer.

The tests passed. We couldn't think of any more test cases. We were done with the nonservlet code. (See Listings 10.7, 10.8, and 10.9.)

LISTING 10.7 Mailer—Refactoring 2

```
public interface Mailer
{
  public boolean send(String to, String subj, String body);
}
```

LISTING 10.8 ForgotPasswordTest—Final Refactoring

```
public class ForgotPasswordTest extends TestCase
{
  public ForgotPasswordTest(String name)
  {
    super(name);
  }

  public static Test suite()
  {
    return new TestSuite(ForgotPasswordTest.class);
  }

  private boolean mailSent;
  private String theToAddr;
  private String theSubj;
  private String theBody;

  public void setup()
  {
    mailSent = false;
    theToAddr = "";
    theSubj = "";
    theBody = "";
  }

  public void testNoUser()
  {
    String noUser = "IDon'tExist";
    PasswordReminderDatabase db =
      new PasswordReminderDatabase()
    {
      public String findPasswordFromEmail(String email)
      {
```

LISTING 10.8 ForgotPasswordTest—Final Refactoring *(continued)*

```
        return null;
      }
    };
    Mailer m = new Mailer()
    {
      public boolean send(String to, String subject,
                          String body)
      {
        mailSent = true;
        return true;
      }
    };
    PasswordReminder pr = new PasswordReminder(db, m);
    assert(pr.remind(noUser) ==
           PasswordReminder.NOEMAILFOUND);
    assert(mailSent == false);
  } // testNoUser

  public void testBadEmail()
  {
    PasswordReminderDatabase db =
      new PasswordReminderDatabase()
    {
      public String findPasswordFromEmail(String email)
      {return "saba";}
    };

    Mailer m = new Mailer()
    {
      public boolean send(String to, String subj,
                          String body)
      {
        theToAddr = to;
        theSubj = subj;
        theBody = body;
        return false;
      }
    };

    PasswordReminder pr = new PasswordReminder(db, m);
    assertEquals(PasswordReminder.EMAILERROR,
                 pr.remind("Bob"));
    assertEquals("Bob", theToAddr);
```

Listing continued on next page.

LISTING 10.8 ForgotPasswordTest—Final Refactoring *(continued)*

```
      assertEquals("Your Object Mentor Password", theSubj);
      assertEquals("Your Object Mentor Password is saba",
                  theBody);
  } // testBadEmail

  public void testGoodEmail()
  {
    PasswordReminderDatabase db =
      new PasswordReminderDatabase()
    {
      public String findPasswordFromEmail(String email)
      {return "saba";}
    };

    Mailer m = new Mailer()
    {
      public boolean send(String to, String subj,
                          String body)
      {
        theToAddr = to;
        theSubj = subj;
        theBody = body;
        return true;
      }
    };

    PasswordReminder pr = new PasswordReminder(db, m);
    assertEquals(PasswordReminder.OK, pr.remind("Bob"));
    assertEquals("Bob", theToAddr);
    assertEquals("Your Object Mentor Password", theSubj);
    assertEquals("Your Object Mentor Password is saba",
                theBody);
  }// testGoodEmail
} // ForgotPasswordTest
```

LISTING 10.9 PasswordReminder—Final Refactoring

```
public class PasswordReminder
{
  public static final int OK = 0;
  public static final int NOEMAILFOUND = 1;
  public static final int EMAILERROR = 2;
```

LISTING 10.9 PasswordReminder—Final Refactoring *(continued)*

```
    private PasswordReminderDatabase itsDb;
    private Mailer itsMailer;
    public PasswordReminder(PasswordReminderDatabase db,
                            Mailer m)
    {
      itsDb = db;
      itsMailer = m;
    }

    public int remind(String email)
    {
      int status = OK;
      String password = itsDb.findPasswordFromEmail(email);
      if (password != null)
      {
        boolean wasSent =
          itsMailer.send(
            email,
            "Your Object Mentor Password",
            "Your Object Mentor Password is " + password);
        if (!wasSent)
          status = EMAILERROR;
      }
      else
        status = NOEMAILFOUND;

      return status;
    }
  }
```

Implementing the Mock-Objects

The Mailer

Next we implemented the two *mock-object* interfaces. The Mailer was quite simple. First we wrote the test cases (Listing 10.10), and then we wrote SMTPMailer (Listing 10.11) to satisfy those test cases.

PasswordReminderDatabase

Implementing the PasswordReminderDatabase was a bit more interesting. The findPasswordFromEmail function already exists in the Database class. The obvious strategy to implementing PasswordReminderDatabase

LISTING 10.10 EmailTest

```
public class EmailTest extends TestCase
{
  public EmailTest(String name)
  {
    super(name);
  }

  public static Test suite()
  {
    return new TestSuite(EmailTest.class);
  }

  public void testBadEmailAddr()
  {
    Mailer m = new SMTPMailer("mail.wwa.com");
    assert(m.send("noAt", "subj", "body")== false);
  }

  public void testBadMailHost()
  {
    Mailer m = new SMTPMailer("wwa.com");
    assert(m.send("newkirk@objectmentor.com", "subj",
                  "body")== false);
  }

  public void testSuccess()
  {
    Mailer m = new SMTPMailer("mail.wwa.com");
    assert(m.send("newkirk@objectmentor.com", "subj",
                  "body")== true);
  }

}
```

is to make Database implement that interface. However, there are two reasons not to do this.

First, we liked the spoofing approach. We envisioned using it quite a bit more in the future. However, we didn't want every spoof to force us to change the Database class.

Second, and more to the point, findUserByEmail is static in Database. You can't put static functions in interfaces.

LISTING 10.11 SMTPMailer

```java
public class SMTPMailer implements Mailer
{
  private String mailHost;

  public SMTPMailer(String mailHost)
  {
    this.mailHost = mailHost;
  }

  public boolean send(String to, String subj, String body)
  {
    boolean sent = true;

    try
    {
      MailMessage msg = new MailMessage(mailHost);
      msg.from("info@objectmentor.com");
      msg.to(to);
      msg.setSubject(subj);

      PrintStream out = msg.getPrintStream();
      out.println(body);
      msg.sendAndClose();
    }
    catch(IOException e)
    {
      e.printStackTrace();
      sent = false;
    }

    return sent;
  }
}
```

So we created an Adapter[1] named PasswordDatabaseAdapter. This class delegated the findUserByEmail function to the static function of Database. (See Listing 10.12)

---

1. Gamma, E., R. Helm, R. Johnson, and J. Vlissides. 1995. *Design patterns: Elements of reusable object-oriented software*. Reading, MA: Addison-Wesley.

LISTING 10.12 PasswordDatabaseAdapter

```
public class PasswordDatabaseAdapter implements
PasswordReminderDatabase
{
  public String findPasswordFromEmail(String email)
  {
    return Database.findPasswordFromEmail(email);
  }
}
```

ForgotPassword Servlet

Finally, still backing into the solution, we wrote the servlet. It's fairly simple, and it creates the necessary objects, invokes remind, and deals with the status. (See Listing 10.13.)

LISTING 10.13 ForgotPassword Servlet

```
public class ForgotPassword extends HttpServlet
{
  private HttpServletRequest request;
  private HttpServletResponse response;
  private String email;
  private String url;

  public void doGet(HttpServletRequest req,
                    HttpServletResponse resp)
    throws ServletException, IOException
  {
    request = req;
    response = resp;
    email = (String)request.getParameter("email");
    url = (String)request.getParameter("url");
    PasswordReminderDatabase db =
      new PasswordDatabaseAdapter();
    Mailer m =
      new SMTPMailer(getInitParameter("mail-server"));
    PasswordReminder pr = new PasswordReminder(db, m);
    int status = pr.remind(email);
    if (status == PasswordReminder.OK)
      redirect("sent");
    else if (status == PasswordReminder.EMAILERROR)
      redirect("bademail");
```

LISTING 10.13 ForgotPassword Servlet (*continued*)

```
      else if (status == PasswordReminder.NOEMAILFOUND)
        redirect("noemail");
  }

  private void redirect(String base)
    throws ServletException, IOException
  {
    String baseURI = getInitParameter(base);
    String uri =
      baseURI + "?email=" + email + "&url=" + url;
    response.sendRedirect(uri);
  }

  public void doPost(HttpServletRequest request,
                     HttpServletResponse response)
    throws ServletException, IOException
  {
    doGet(request, response);
  }
}
```

There appears to be some duplication between this servlet and `RedirectingServlet`. We leave that refactoring as an exercise for the reader ;).

Conclusion

After we got the servlet in place, we ran our manual acceptance tests. Everything worked as planned.

The total time spent on this task was about four hours instead of the six that we had estimated.

The most important lesson learned in this task was the practice of backing into solutions from initial premises and constraints. The technique of using mock-objects to keep all the test-related information inside the test cases was very useful and also helped us maintain our backwards thinking.

Tracking

Table 10.1 describes the tasks that have been completed with the actual values.

TABLE 10.1 Current Tracking Information

Task	Programmer	Estimate (ideal hours)	Actual hours
Task 6.1: *Login Start*	Jim	4	Not started
Task 6.2: *Login Page HTML*	Jim	4	Not started
Task 6.3: *Login Task*	Jim	8	8
Task 6.4: *Enter as Guest Task*	Bob	4	1.5
Task 6.5: *Forgot Password Task*	Bob	6	4
Task 6.6: *Create Database Task*	Jim	8	4
Task 6.7: *Registration HTML*	Bob	4	Not started
Task 6.8: *Registration Task Servlet*	Bob	8	Not started
Task 6.9: *Reset Servlet Task*	Jim	4	Not started
Total		50	17.5

Chapter 11

Infrastructure Thrashing

We started doing Task 6.8: *Registration Task Servlet*. This task receives data from the registration form, adds the user to the database, and sends the user e-mail with his or her password.

The first thing we thought about was adding the user to the database. We had written a simple `addUser` function on page 56 as part of our anticipated infrastructure (See Listing 11.1.). Now we had to make it work in the real application.

This `addUser` function took a naive approach to error processing. Several things could go wrong during `addUser`. Some were unexpected, such as failure to connect to the database or a hardware failure. Others were expected, such as a malformed e-mail address (key) or attempting to add a user that already exists in the database.

Unfortunately, `addUser` dealt with all of these problems by throwing `SQLException`. Throwing an exception is appropriate when something unexpected happens, such as being unable to connect to the database. On the other hand, throwing an exception for duplicate keys is pretty ugly. It's not wise to throw exceptions for normal error conditions; it is better to return a status.

This point was driven home as we wrote the test cases for registration. Duplicate e-mail addresses were something we expected to happen during normal operation. Users who had forgotten that they had registered might simply reregister. (This was User Story 4.11: *Existing User*.)

LISTING 11.1 Database.addUser

```
public void addUser(User u) throws SQLException
{
  Statement statement = con.createStatement();

  statement.executeUpdate(
    "INSERT INTO userlist VALUES " +
    "('" + u.getEmailAddress() + "','" +
    u.getPassword() + "','" +
    u.getOrganization() + "','" +
    u.getFirstName() + "','" +
    u.getLastName() + "'," +
    u.getNotification() + ")");
}
```

There was an existing test called testAdd in DatabaseAccessTest. (See Listing 11.2.) But this test case did not try to add a duplicate record. To detect a duplicate record we could call findUserByEmail before calling addUser. However, this is fairly expensive because it's doing a lot of work to check for something that won't happen very often.

LISTING 11.2 DatabaseAccessTest.testAdd

```
public void testAdd() throws Exception
{
    String email = "123@universe.com";
    User u = new User(email,
      "456",
      "First",
      "Last",
      "The Universe",
      false);

    assert(db.findUserByEmail(email) == null);

    db.addUser(u);

    User dbUser = db.findUserByEmail(email);
    assert(dbUser != null);
    assertEquals(u, dbUser);

    db.deleteUser( email );
    assert( db.findUserByEmail( email ) == null );
}
```

This implied that we should call `addUser` and catch the exception that would be thrown upon a duplicate. This is not how we wanted the test case to look. Rather, we wanted the test case to have a nice "if" statement that checked for the duplicate case. That is we wanted:

```
if (db.addUser(user) == false)
    // duplicate
```

Rather than:

```
try
{
    db.addUser(user)
}
catch(SQLException e)
{
    // duplicate
}
```

Aside from the pleasant terseness of the former code, it also doesn't depend upon `SQLException`. We didn't want the application code and servlets depending on details of the database. Therefore we wrote a new test case named `testDuplicate`, as shown in Listing 11.3.

Of course this didn't compile; so we had to change `addUser` in order to not throw exceptions. (See Listing 11.4.)

LISTING 11.3 DatabaseAccessTest.testDuplicate

```
public void testDuplicate() throws Exception
{
    String email1 = "idiott@universe.com";
    User user1 = new User(email1,
        "456",
        "First",
        "Last",
        "The Universe",
        false);
    assert(db.findUserByEmail(email1) == null);
    assert(db.addUser(user1) == true);
    assert(db.addUser(user1) == false);

    db.deleteUser( email1 );
    assert( db.findUserByEmail( email1 ) == null );
}
```

LISTING 11.4 `Database.addUser`

```
public boolean addUser(User u)
{
  try
  {
    Statement statement = con.createStatement();

    statement.executeUpdate("INSERT INTO userlist VALUES "+
                            "('" + u.getEmailAddress() +
                            "','" +
                            u.getPassword() + "','" +
                            u.getOrganization() + "','" +
                            u.getFirstName() + "','" +
                            u.getLastName() + "'," +
                            u.getNotification() + ")");
  }
  catch (Exception e)
  {
    return false;
  }

  return true;
}
```

As you can see, we decided to bundle all possible failures into the return status. For more elaborate applications, this would be inappropriate. But for this iteration it was sufficient.

Refactoring the Tests

Notice that the setup code in `DatabaseAccessTest.testAdd` (Listing 11.2) and `DatabaseAccessTest.testDuplicate` (Listing 11.3) are very similar. We wanted to refactor the redundancy out of them. We could do this by extracting the setup code into its own method. However, JUnit already has a feature that supports common setup code. Unfortunately, the setup code for the other tests in `DatabaseAccessTest` is not the same. So we decided to break `testDuplicate` and `testAdd` out into their own test case class named `DatabaseAddTest`. (See Listing 11.5.)

LISTING 11.5 DatabaseAddTest

```
import junit.framework.*;

public class DatabaseAddTest extends TestCase
{
  private Database db;
  private User user1;
  private String email1 = "123@universe.com";

  public DatabaseAddTest(String name)
  {
    super(name);
  }

  public static Test suite()
  {
    return new TestSuite(DatabaseAddTest.class);
  }


  protected void setUp() throws Exception
  {
    user1 = new User(email1,
      "456",
      "First",
      "Last",
      "The Universe",
      false);
    db = new Database("websiteusers");
    db.open();
  }

  protected void tearDown() throws Exception
  {
    db.close();
  }

  public void testAdd() throws Exception
  {
    assert(db.findUserByEmail(email1) == null);
    assert(db.addUser(user1) == true);
```

Listing continued on next page.

LISTING 11.5 DatabaseAddTest (*continued*)

```
      User dbUser = db.findUserByEmail(email1);
      assert(dbUser != null);
      assertEquals(user1, dbUser);

      db.deleteUser( email1 );
      assert( db.findUserByEmail( email1 ) == null );
   }

   public void testDuplicate() throws Exception
   {
      assert(db.findUserByEmail(email1) == null);
      assert(db.addUser(user1) == true);
      assert(db.addUser(user1) == false);

      db.deleteUser( email1 );
      assert( db.findUserByEmail( email1 ) == null );
   }

}
```

Refactoring the Database—Again

In order for the registration servlet to call Database.addUser, it had to create a database object and open it. It also had to make sure that the database object was closed when it was done. We can see this pattern in the validateLogin function in Listing 8.10 on page 73.

Notice that validateLogin does not use any of the instance variables of the Database class. It could be static! Clearly a similar static add function could also be created. This would keep all the database management code out of the application. Indeed, it appeared to us that the interface between the application and the database *always* should be through these static functions. These functions would manage the database connection and assume that the objects being manipulated were User objects. Thus was born the UserDatabase class.

First, we moved the test cases for the add and validateLogin functions to a new class named DatabaseStaticTest. (See Listing 11.6.) These functions needed a bit of refactoring. They now needed to invoke static functions to add, delete, and find users.

Next we wrote the UserDatabase class with all the static functions required by the test case. (See Listing 11.7.)

LISTING 11.6 DatabaseStaticTest

```java
import junit.framework.*;

public class DatabaseStaticTest extends TestCase
{
  private User user1;
  private String email1 = "123@universe.com";

  public DatabaseStaticTest(String name)
  {
    super(name);
  }

  public static Test suite()
  {
    return new TestSuite(DatabaseStaticTest.class);
  }

  protected void setUp() throws Exception
  {
    user1 = new User(email1,
      "456",
      "First",
      "Last",
      "The Universe",
      false);
  }

  public void testAdd() throws Exception
  {
    assert(UserDatabase.findUser(email1) == null);
    assert(UserDatabase.add(user1) == true);

    User dbUser = UserDatabase.findUser(email1);
    assert(dbUser != null);
    assertEquals(user1, dbUser);

    assert(UserDatabase.delete(email1));
    assert(UserDatabase.findUser(email1) == null);
  }

  public void testDuplicate() throws Exception
  {
    assert(UserDatabase.findUser(email1) == null);
    assert(UserDatabase.add(user1) == true);
```

Listing continued on next page.

LISTING 11.6 DatabaseStaticTest *(continued)*

```
      assert(UserDatabase.add(user1) == false);

      assert(UserDatabase.delete(email1));
      assert(UserDatabase.findUser(email1) == null);
   }

   public void testValidateLogin() throws Exception
   {
      assert(UserDatabase.validateLogin(
            "newkirk@objectmentor.com", "jim"));
      assert(!UserDatabase.validateLogin(
            "123@objectmentor.com", "test"));
      assert(!UserDatabase.validateLogin("", "test"));
      assert(!UserDatabase.validateLogin(
            "newkirk@objectmentor.com", "test"));
      assert(!UserDatabase.validateLogin(null, null));
   }
}
```

LISTING 11.7 UserDatabase

```
import java.sql.*;

public class UserDatabase
{

   public static User findUser(String email) throws Error
   {
      User result = null;

      Database db = null;
      try
      {
         db = new Database("websiteusers");
         db.open();

         result = db.findUserByEmail(email);
      }
      catch(SQLException e)
      {}
      finally
      {
         try
         { if(db != null) db.close();}
```

LISTING 11.7 UserDatabase *(continued)*

```
      catch(SQLException e)
      {}

  }
  return result;
}

public static boolean validateLogin(String email,
                                    String password)
{
  boolean result = false;

  Database db = null;
  try
  {
    db = new Database("websiteusers");
    db.open();

    User u = db.findUserByEmail(email);
    if( u != null)
    {
      result = u.validate(password);

    }
  }
  catch(SQLException e)
  {}
  finally
  {
    try
    { if(db != null) db.close();}
    catch(SQLException e)
    {}

  }
  return result;
}

public static boolean add(User newUser) throws Error
{
  boolean result = false;

  Database db = null;
  try
```

Listing continued on next page.

LISTING 11.7 UserDatabase (*continued*)

```
      {
        db = new Database("websiteusers");
        db.open();

        result = db.addUser(newUser);
      }
      catch(SQLException e)
      {}
      finally
      {
        try
        { if(db != null) db.close();}
        catch(SQLException e)
        {}

      }
      return result;
    }

    public static boolean delete(String email) throws Error
    {
      boolean result = false;

      Database db = null;
      try
      {
        db = new Database("websiteusers");
        db.open();

        result = db.deleteUser(email);
      }
      catch(SQLException e)
      {}
      finally
      {
        try
        { if(db != null) db.close();}
        catch(SQLException e)
        {}

      }

      return result;
    }
}
```

This class worked, but was big and full of duplicated code. Indeed, much of the code was created with cut and paste.[1] Clearly, some additional refactoring was required.

We realized that every function is composed of three parts. The first part makes sure the database is opened correctly. The second part does the needed function. The third part makes sure the database gets closed properly. We extracted the first and last parts into special functions in UserDatabase and then called those extracted functions. The result is in Listing 11.8.

LISTING 11.8 UserDatabase—Refactoring 1

```java
import java.sql.*;

public class UserDatabase
{
  public static Database open() throws Error
  {
    Database db = null;
    try
    {
        db = new Database("websiteusers");
        db.open();
    }
    catch (SQLException e)
    {
        throw new Error(e.toString());
    }
    return db;
  }

  public static void close(Database db) throws Error
  {
    try
    { if(db != null) db.close();}
    catch(SQLException e)
    { throw new Error(e.toString()); }
  }
```

Listing continued on next page.

---

1. An early, and still prevalent, reuse mechanism.

LISTING 11.8 UserDatabase—Refactoring 1 (*continued*)

```
    public static User findUser(String email) throws Error
    {
      Database db = open();
      User result = db.findUserByEmail(email);
      close(db);
      return result;
    }

    public static boolean validateLogin(String email,
                                        String password)
    {
      boolean result = false;

      Database db = open();
      User u = db.findUserByEmail(email);
      if( u != null)
          result = u.validate(password);
      close(db);
      return result;
    }

    public static boolean add(User newUser) throws Error
    {
      Database db = open();
      boolean result = db.addUser(newUser);
      close(db);
      return result;
    }

    public static boolean delete(String email) throws Error
    {
      Database db = open();
      boolean result = db.deleteUser(email);
      close(db);
      return result;
    }
  }
```

This is much nicer. Each of the functions is easier to read and understand, and there is no duplicated code. Moreover, through all this refactoring, the tests remained unchanged and working.

Infrastructure Revolution

The way the application interfaces to the database is remarkably different from the infrastructure we anticipated on page 48. Had we resisted the temptation to build that infrastructure early and instead used the spoofing technique (see page 92), we may have come up with similar results without the stress and two hours of thrashing.

The Registration Servlet

The code for the registration servlet is shown in Listing 11.9. It is fairly straightforward. The PasswordGenerator class simply generates a random eight-character password. Its implementation is not particularly interesting and is left to the reader as an exercise.[2]

LISTING 11.9 RegistrationServlet.java

```java
import java.io.*;
import javax.servlet.*;
import javax.servlet.http.*;
import com.oreilly.servlet.*;

public class RegistrationServlet extends HttpServlet
{
  private HttpServletRequest itsRequest;
  private HttpServletResponse itsResponse;
  private String email;

  public void doGet(HttpServletRequest request,
                    HttpServletResponse response)
    throws ServletException, IOException
  {
    itsRequest = request;
    itsResponse = response;

      String firstName =
        itsRequest.getParameter("firstname");
```

Listing continued on next page.

---

2. You have 30 seconds, beginning now.

LISTING 11.9 RegistrationServlet.java (*continued*)

```
      String lastName =
        itsRequest.getParameter("lastname");
      String organization =
        itsRequest.getParameter("organization");
      email = itsRequest.getParameter("emailAddress");
      String password =
        PasswordGenerator.generatePassword();

      boolean notify = true;
      String stringNotify =
        itsRequest.getParameter("notification");
      if(stringNotify == null)
        notify = false;

    User user = new User( email,
                    password,
                    firstName,
                    lastName,
                    organization,
                    notify);
    boolean success = UserDatabase.add(user);
    if (success)
    {
        if (mailPassword(email, password))
            redirect("success");
        else
        {
            UserDatabase.delete(email);
            redirect("mailfailure");
        }
    }
    else
    {
        redirect("addfailure");
    }
  }

  private boolean mailPassword(String email,
                               String password)
  {
      Mailer m = new SMTPMailer(
                    getInitParameter("mail-server"));
      boolean wasSent =
        m.send(email,"Your Object Mentor Password",
                    "Your Object Mentor Password is " +
                    password);
      return wasSent;
```

LISTING 11.9 RegistrationServlet.java (*continued*)

```java
    }

    private void redirect(String base)
      throws ServletException, IOException
    {
      String url = (String)itsRequest.getParameter("url");
      String baseURI = getInitParameter(base);
      String uri = baseURI + "?email=" + email + "&url=" +
                    url;
       itsResponse.sendRedirect(uri);
     }

    private void redirect()
      throws ServletException, IOException
    {
      String url = (String)itsRequest.getParameter("url");
      if(url == null)
        url = getInitParameter("home");
      itsResponse.sendRedirect(url);
    }

    public void doPost(HttpServletRequest request,
                       HttpServletResponse response)
      throws ServletException, IOException
    {
      doGet(request, response);
    }
  }
```

Conclusion

Anticipating the structure of the database in the early part of the iteration didn't do us much good. As we developed the servlets, we found
that they were hard to test, and so we needed to drive as much functionality out of them as we could. So, we wanted to isolate the servlets
as much as possible from the database stuff. This led us to alter the way
the servlets interfaced to the database significantly.

Also, creating the database infrastructure early gave us a false sense of
security. We thought we had it all figured out. It wasn't until later in the
iteration, when the constraints surrounding the servlets were much
clearer, that we discovered our initial design was lacking.

It is hard to go back and predict what might have happened if we had used the spoofing technique in the early phases of the iteration and then built the database at the very end. But one thing is clear: We would have known what the issues were. And there *were* issues we were unaware of at the start.

Refactoring the database took four hours. Completing the `Registration Servlet`, including the HTML (Task 6.8: *Registration Task Servlet* and Task 6.7: *Registration HTML*), took another four hours. They were estimated at eight and four hours, respectively.

It would seem that our estimates were conservative. On the other hand, refactoring the database was not anticipated and took just as long as the servlet. Had our estimates been more accurate, this refactoring would have been costly.

Tracking

Table 11.1 describes the tasks that have been completed with the actual times.

TABLE 11.1 Current Tracking Information

Task	Programmer	Estimate (ideal hours)	Actual hours
Task 6.1: *Login Start*	Jim	4	Not started
Task 6.2: *Login Page HTML*	Jim	4	Not started
Task 6.3: *Login Task*	Jim	8	8
Task 6.4: *Enter as Guest Task*	Bob	4	1.5
Task 6.5: *Forgot Password Task*	Bob	6	4
Task 6.6: *Create Database Task*	Jim	8	4
Task 6.7: *Registration HTML*	Bob	4	4
Task 6.8: *Registration Task Servlet*	Bob	8	8
Task 6.9: *Reset Servlet Task*	Jim	4	Not started
Total		50	29.5

Chapter 12

Iteration 1—Summary

After 39.5 hours of work, the iteration came to an end. The tests were working, and the manual acceptance tests all passed. Lowell had not seen the result yet, but we were confident he would be pleased.

Table 12.1, on the following page, shows the actual hours spent on each task in this iteration. Note that in most instances our estimates were too conservative.

Cookie Woes

Task 6.9: *Reset Servlet Task* was problematic for several reasons. It was defined on page 42 within the context of the login task. It allows users to erase the current cookie on their machine and replace it with a new one.

The ability to erase a cookie was convenient for our manual acceptance tests. Often one of the steps in these test procedures was to erase the current cookie. It would have been possible to erase the cookie manually by going into the cookie folder and deleting the cookie file, but because we had to write *Reset Servlet Task* anyway, we incorporated it into the acceptance tests instead.

TABLE 12.1 Actual Hours Spent on Tasks in Iteration 1

Task	Programmer	Estimate (ideal hours)	Actual hours
Task 6.1: *Login Start*	Jim	4	4
Task 6.2: *Login Page HTML*	Jim	4	3
Task 6.3: *Login Task*	Jim	8	8
Task 6.4: *Enter as Guest Task*	Bob	4	1.5
Task 6.5: *Forgot Password Task*	Bob	6	4
Task 6.6: *Create Database Task*	Jim	8	4
Task 6.7: *Registration HTML*	Bob	4	4
Task 6.8: *Registration Task Servlet*	Bob	8	4
Task 6.9: *Reset Servlet Task*	Jim	4	7
Total		50	39.5

Our first problem was purely technical. Although the documentation surrounding cookies provided what appeared to be an easy way to erase them, it turned out that some browsers did not obey those conventions.

We started with a very naive assumption. The documents told us that if you set the maxAge parameter of a cookie to –1, the cookie would be deleted. So we wrote the following code:

```
if (name.equals("email")){
  c.setMaxAge(-1);
  response.addCookie(c);
  return;
}
```

This didn't work in all browsers. In some browsers the cookie remained. We didn't understand why, so we punted by trying to erase the contents of the cookie.

```
if (name.equals("email")){
  c.setValue("");
  c.setMaxAge(-1);
```

```
    response.addCookie(c);
    return;
}
```

However, the cookie remained! What was going on? We spent a long time trying to figure this out, which is why this task took so much longer than it was supposed to. For several hours we were stymied.

Then Jim, while trying random tactics, stumbled upon the following:

```
if (name.equals("email")){
  c.setValue("");
  c.setMaxAge(-1);
  c.setPath("/");
  response.addCookie(c);
  return;
}
```

Urg! It appears that one very popular browser does not send the path variable of the cookie and does not recognize changes to the cookie unless the path variable has been set to the same value it had when it was created.

We found no documents that warned us about this. Had we not gotten lucky with our random tactics, there's no telling how long it would have taken us to solve it.[1]

The second problem we had with this task was that in the middle of the iteration, Lowell changed his mind about a few things. While we were clarifying how the login screen was going to work, Lowell decided that the best way for a user to delete the cookie was described in User Story 4.5: *Smart Site Header*. Because this story was not in the current release, Lowell decided not to bother with deleting cookies in this iteration.

This left us with a task that had no story behind it. Unfortunately we had already written the ResetServlet and gotten it to work. Had we known that Lowell wasn't going to want this feature, we could have erased the cookies manually in the acceptance tests.

---

1. Actually, we are not convinced that it works reliably. During our manual testing, it sometimes happened that the cookie apparently did not get erased. It remains something of a mystery.

HTML/JSP Tasks

The HTML/JSP tasks were straightforward. We used our graphic artist to help us create HTML with the appropriate look and feel. Then we converted the HTML to JSP.

We have seen JSP systems in which a lot of Java and HTML are mixed together. These systems are typically a mess. The mixture of HTML with loops, nested loops, and extended conditionals is extremely difficult to read and maintain.

Our goal was to minimize the amount of Java that appeared in the JSPs. We restricted ourselves to simple Java statements that accessed parameters in the application.[2] For example:

```
<input type=hidden name="url"
       value="<%=request.getParameter("url")%>">
```

We Thought We Were Done

Lowell had not seen the iteration yet, but we were confident that all was in accord with his expectations. We set up a meeting with him to go over the iteration and to plan the next iteration. That meeting was to take place the following Monday.

For the complete source code for the iteration see Appendix A: Iteration 1—Source Code.

---

2. Nowadays (four months later ;^)), this separation of content and presentation would be better done with XML/XSLT.

Chapter 13

Steering

*A mature organization does not
abandon its process in a crisis.*
—Watts Humphreys

At the end of the iteration, Lowell sat down with us to review and
accept the results. He had not written any acceptance tests of his own,
so he used ours instead. He sat down and played with the software a bit
and found some things he didn't like.

- ✧ In the header of every page having to do with login and registration, there is a sentence that reads: "Click here for more information." Lowell had added this in the midst of the iteration while
  helping us define how the pages should look. When you clicked
  on this sentence, it took you to the objectmentor.com home page
  as a stopgap measure until the actual help page could be written.
  Lowell said he would write the help page and wanted the link to
  be changed.

- ✧ During registration, if there was a problem sending e-mail to the
  entered address, the system would take you to a page that
  informed you of the failure and asked you to "Click here to try
  again." When you clicked, it took you back to the registration
  form, with all the fields empty. Lowell wanted the fields to be
  filled with the data from the previous registration attempt.

- ✧ Lowell didn't like the format of the registration form. He wanted
  it to take up less vertical space, and he wanted some of the word-
  ing changed.

- The e-mail that the system sent to the registering user was terse. Our old system had a nicely formatted letter that gave the recipient the password and pointed to URLs containing our site policies. Lowell asked us to move that letter into the new system.

- When a user registers, the system e-mails the new password to the user and takes him or her to the confirmation page that tells the user to wait for the e-mail message and then "Click here." When the user clicks, the system takes him or her to the login page with the e-mail address already loaded. Lowell wanted this changed so that a user could log in directly from the confirmation page. He wanted to add all the fields of the login page to the end of the confirmation page, all loaded and ready to go. All users would have to do is type their password and click on the login button.

Lowell wrote new stories for all his concerns and asked us to estimate them. We estimated these stories in Lowell's presence. The cards, with their estimates, appear in User Stories 13.1 through 13.5.

As you can see, all these stories were between one and four hours. They totaled to 10 hours altogether. Thus the first 40-hour iteration generated about 25% rework. It's good to learn this early as opposed to much later. Having gotten this feedback, we had a better understanding of the kinds of things that Lowell wanted. Also, it was good to see that Lowell was happy with the overall operation of the system. Aside from the cosmetic details mentioned in the new stories, we were building the right system.

Change link to "click for additional information" to a member FAQ/Overview page.

(Lowell to deliver page.)

One hour

USER STORY 13.1 Click for Overview

On the "there was a problem sending to . . ." page, the "click here to try again!" link should return to the registration form with the data filled in (i.e., = Back).

Four hours

USER STORY 13.2 Back with Filled Fields

Registration page screen changes.
– Smaller line breaks.
– Change "add to mailing list" explanation.
Lowell will provide new text.

One hour

USER STORY 13.3 Registration Page Cosmetics

The registration confirmation e-mail should be identical to the e-mail message in the current (legacy) registration system.

One hour

USER STORY 13.4 Registration E-mail

USER STORY 13.5 Combine Confirmation and Login

Finding and correcting problems early is one of the goals of steering. It prevents errors from accumulating and code being built upon incorrect assumptions.

Having said all this, redoing 25% of the stories in a one-week iteration is disappointing. Looking back on it, we should have insisted that Lowell be much more involved than he was. We also should have insisted that he provide, or at least help us write, acceptance tests. Steering is valuable, but even in a one-week iteration steering is not a replacement for an on-site customer.

An Interesting Misunderstanding

Sometime before the end of the first iteration, Lowell was tasked by his boss (Bob) to get lots of people registered on the Web site as soon as possible. The reason for this was to create an e-mail list to announce new public courses and other offerings.

Over the years, more than 11,000 people had left their e-mail addresses with us. We did not want to simply add these e-mail addresses to a regular mailing list; we felt this would be "spamming" them. But we were comfortable sending one e-mail to these people inviting them to register on our Web site and receive regular e-mail announcements from us.

Lowell asked us to take the first iteration partially live when it was complete. His intent was to include the URL of the registration page in the invitation e-mail. The invited guests could then click on that URL to register, and they would be added to our database.

We agreed to this plan because the registration page would be done and working by the end of the iteration. In retrospect this was a bad idea.

We took Lowell's request to mean that there would be no change to the *existing* Web site. Recipients of the e-mail would use the URL it contained and would be able to register with the new software. But none of the rest of the new software would be available to them, nor would they have access to it from the existing Web site. The existing Web site would continue to use the old registration software.

When the registration software was ready, we asked Lowell if there was anything else we needed to do before the e-mail was sent. He replied: "It's not live; it's not integrated into the Web site. It says 'XP in Practice' and not 'Object Mentor' on all the pages." This was the beginning of a miscommunication that would go on for some time. The following is a transcript of the discussion that took place:

(Discussing the graphic at the top of the pages, which currently says "XP in Practice" and not "Object Mentor.")

Lowell: I'm OK with adding a requirement that says the pages exist in two forms: One for XP in Practice and the other for Object Mentor.

Jim: Then you should write a story that says integrate it into the Object Mentor Web site. That's going to take more than one or two days.

Lowell: To change a graphic on the top of the page?

Jim: No, to integrate it into the Object Mentor Web site.

Lowell: None of these stories (referring to the first iteration) are done until they are working on the live site.

Jim: It is working on the live site.

Lowell: No it is not. The way you register at *objectmenor.com* does not touch any of this code.

Jim: That was never one of the stories.

Lowell: It's the premise of the entire project!

Jim: Then you'd better write a story for it.

Lowell: That's equivalent to writing a story that says "come to work at 9 AM."

Jim: No it's not. You want an e-mail message that has a link to the place to register.

Lowell: We have that story; it's right here [pointing to something]. What you are telling me is that this is done even though it's not live on the site. It's like telling me it's done because it's running on your laptop. That's not done! This is the definition of a release.

Jim: Yeah, and an iteration is not a release.

Lowell: Well, it can be.

Jim: It is not, based on our discussion, which was that three iterations make one release.

Lowell: No, that's not true because a little while ago I said to you: We have this project to e-mail out to people to notify them of our classes.

Jim: And you told me that all you needed was the registration page, which is there.

Lowell: It's not there!

Jim: It is too there!

Lowell: It's not live!

Jim: It's live on the Internet.

Lowell: Oh, so you're telling me I can put in this e-mail, this other link.

Jim: I can put any link into the e-mail.

Lowell: [Pause] OK. Please write here the URL of the link that I can put into the e-mail.

Jim: [Writes the link on a card and hands it to Lowell.]

Lowell: That's going to get me to the registration page?

Jim: Yep.

Lowell: OK. Alright; alright. Fair enough. Yep, OK.

Jim: That's what you told me.

Lowell: N-n-n-n-no, that's fine. Yep . . . yep, yep, yep, yep, yep.

Jim: So the question is: do you want the graphic changed?

Lowell: Ah, right! So rewinding back past all that anxiety, it's a graphic change . . .

Jim: . . . if its just that . . .

Lowell: . . . but you said it would take . . .

Jim: . . . N-n-n-no, YOU said take the membership area and . . .

Lowell: . . . yeah, yeah, yeah, yeah, yeah . . .

Jim: . . . make this the membership area of the Web site.

Lowell: Well, I can do that! If I have this link, then I can do that. And it's not two or three days, it's an hour. I can take the Login button from the home page, and I can redirect that to this link you gave me.

Jim: Right; but there's no navigation and stuff on any of those things . . .

Lowell: . . . but I can do that . . .

Jim: . . . Okay, great, wonderful . . .

Lowell: I'd rather have you guys do that, but if you're going to give me a three-day estimate, I'm going to do it myself.

Jim: I asked what you wanted, and it is completely ambiguous to me what you want. So I'm not even going to estimate what you asked for.

Lowell: Nothing is done until it's live on *objectmentor.com*, and I don't need to write a story that says "this stuff has to be real."

Jim: But to play back the story, it requires all three iterations to be done.

Lowell: Absolutely true; you're right. We're talking about releasing an iteration, which is not what we planned.

Jim: And you are only talking about releasing one of the pages of the iteration, which is the registration page.

Lowell: But once you do that, you can hit all the other pages.

Jim: Yes, but we're not saying we'd actually go back and change the Web site to change all that stuff.

Lowell: Yes, true, true.

Clearly there was some angst and miscommunication going on, though it appears that Jim and Lowell settled the issue.

What Went Wrong?

The fundamental miscommunication was over the definition of the early release that Lowell wanted. Jim thought that Lowell wanted to send an e-mail message with a link to a stand-alone page. This was partially correct. But Lowell also wanted to be able to get to the registration page from the *objectmentor.com* home page. His way of saying this was: "It needs to be live." Being "live" had a different meaning to Jim. He estimated that as several days' worth of work. Lowell's response was to claim he could do it in a few hours.

This is a microcosm of much larger troubles between development and business. In the preceding confrontation, we see all of the angst, ire, posturing, and stonewalling that also can occur in larger projects. We even saw the customer making estimates for the developers and the developers assuming business value for the customer. It is a classic blurring of the lines between business and development that XP strives to solve.

And what caused it? A change in business priority. The original plan did not have the registration system going live until the end of the third iteration. However, a very real change in business priorities forced Lowell to try to get part of the project released early. Lowell and Jim communicated this verbally, but no story was written and no estimates were made.

Had a story been written and estimated as XP recommends, the miscommunication would have been discovered much earlier. The gross difference between the cost that Lowell expected and Jim estimated would have driven the conversation at a time when stress levels were not so high.

Thus it is very important that scheduling decisions be made in the context of both a story and an estimate. Our real failure was to abandon our process because of a priority (crisis). A coach would have spotted our error and corrected it.

During the process, we didn't have an on-site customer. Had Lowell been seeing progress on a day-by-day basis, this issue would have been spotted earlier and resolved *within* the iteration. There would have been no surprise at the end.

However, because there was no consistent communication with Lowell, we fell into the "it ain't my job" mindset. We took the stories literally and refused to accept responsibility for Lowell's disappointment at the end. This is the definition of an unhealthy project.

As developers, we should have sought Lowell's involvement much more actively. We should have scheduled meetings with him and forced him to see what we were doing. We should have taken responsibility (or at least our share of it) for maintaining the collaborative mindset.

Lowell had something to say about this too. See *Being Engaged*.

Words of the Customer

Being Engaged

So, where was I? Jim and I had developed projects together many times in the past. I have always known Jim to rise over any obstacle to deliver the software that his customer needed. In our effort to use XP as purely as possible, Jim fought off his temptation to steer, leaving that responsibility to me, his customer. As the business priority for this application changed, I reverted to my old mindset and just assumed that Jim would do the driving for me and focused on other priorities. The problem was Jim had no way of knowing what my priorities were without my participation.

Traditionally, business people have been able to rely on technical people making business decisions. Engineers have been rewarded for taking a vague set of requirements and "making the magic happen." Business people then had the luxury to let the engineers do the legwork for the business. This was feasible in relatively static environments. In an environment of rapid change, it is not possible for engineers to track the changing business priorities and the technologies that are required to develop innovative products. Business must be engaged in order to steer the project if the end result is going to align with their needs and priorities. So, as we start our XP projects, we need to ensure that we have a customer in place that is empowered and has the time available to steer the project and specify acceptance tests.

In this case, a little more of my participation or a few test cases would have flushed out the disconnect and accelerated delivery of what I needed.

Chapter 14

Finishing the Release

We all have the extraordinary code within us,
waiting to be released.

—Jean Houston

Now we will move quickly through the rest of this story. The next two iterations proceeded with very few problems, and a detailed description would yield few new insights. So this chapter will just describe the highlights.

For the second iteration, we completely swapped out the programming staff. The programmers on the first iteration were too busy with other responsibilities to continue. For the project to move forward without continual interruption, we decided to have Chris and Micah, two of our developers, take the place of Bob and Jim.

Chris and Micah had already established a velocity of 3.25 on other projects. However, because they had to come up to speed on the new code, we lowered it to 2.5. This meant that Chris and Micah could do five days' worth of stories in the second iteration.

Lowell picked stories for the iteration. Table 14.1, on the following page, shows his choice.

Can't You Fit Two Hours?

The stories that Lowell chose added up to more than the five days that Chris and Micah could do in one iteration. So, Lowell had to remove

TABLE 14.1 Stories Chosen for Iteration 2

Story	Estimate
User Story 4.11: *Existing User*	1 day
User Story 4.19: *Changing User Profile*	2 days
User Story 4.16: *Notification Specialization*	1 day
User Story 13.1: *Click for Overview*	1 hour
User Story 13.2: *Back with Filled Fields*	4 hours
User Story 13.3: *Registration Page Cosmetics*	1 hour
User Story 13.4: *Registration E-mail*	1 hour
User Story 13.5: *Combine Confirmation and Login*	3 hours
Total	42 hours

something. He removed User Story 13.2: *Back with Filled Fields* from the plan and substituted a stopgap solution, written on a new card, named User Story 14.1: *Click Back*. Rather than guarantee that all the fields were filled with previously entered data, Lowell was happy simply to tell the user to click "Back."

We realized that we could clip this story to User Story: 13.3: *Registration Page Cosmetics* without increasing the estimate. The story was simply the addition of text to a page, which was what *Registration Page Cosmetics* was all about anyway.

This brought the total down from 42 hours to 38. Lowell was happy with this.

USER STORY 14.1 Click Back

Task Planning

Chris and Micah broke the stories into tasks and estimated them. The estimates totaled up to 31 hours. So, we went back to Lowell and asked him if there was anything he wanted to add. He immediately reinstated User Story 13.2: *Back with Filled Fields* and cancelled User Story 14.1: *Click Back. C'est la guerre.*

The Iteration

Jim spent three hours working with Chris and Micah on one of the tasks in User Story 4.16: *Notification Specialization*. Jim was able to show the overall structure of the code to them and get them moving on the project.

The Change Process

We had learned some lessons from the previous iteration. Jim communicated those lessons to Chris and Micah by example. He showed them the way we had learned to make changes to a Web application. (See Figure 14.1.)

Given a new feature or a change to an existing feature, we learned to perform the following steps:

1. Change the HTML so that it shows what you want. Remember to check this with the customer frequently.
2. Write a test that drives the nonservlet code and will pass when that code implements the new feature.
3. Change the nonservlet code, including the database if necessary, until the test passes.
4. The test drives the nonservlet code, so it is a model of what the servlet code needs to look like. Make changes to the servlet based upon that model.

Steps 2 and 3 are recursive. As you change the nonservlet code to make the test pass, you likely will find that you need to write another test, at a lower-level. You will make this lower-level test pass before you can make the original test pass.

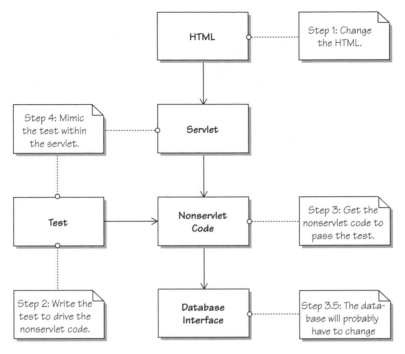

FIGURE 14.1 How we changed our Web application

In this sense, test-first programming has a stacklike structure. You may find yourself needing to pass a low-level test before you can pass a mid-level test needed to pass a high-level test.

Concluding Iteration 2

After the initial three hours of Jim's time, Chris and Micah were on their own. Despite their being thrown into a new project with a minimum of guidance, the iteration went very well. Chris and Micah brought the iteration to a close within the allotted time. Indeed, their actual velocity turned out to be about 2.9, a little better than expected.

Lessons Learned

We lost the whole development team! This is the disaster scenario that so many project managers fear. The production of up-front documentation is often used to allay these fears. In our case the tests, and three hours with Jim, took the place of that documentation.

Clearly, this was a tiny amount of code, and any reasonable team could have come up to speed on it within short order. Even so, the team was *completely exchanged* without visible loss of productivity. Indeed, the team managed to do better than their initial estimates.

The thrashing over User Story 13.2: *Back with Filled Fields* might seem excessive. However, the alternative would have been to commit to too much too early. We had tried that in the first iteration and did not like the outcome. In this case, we met our commitments. The customer got what he wanted when we said he would get it.

The Third Iteration

To close the second iteration, Lowell needed to accept it. To accept it, he had to run all the manual acceptance tests. This turned out to be very time consuming for him.

To make matters worse, Lowell was not the author of the manual acceptance tests. So when he *did* run them, he found that they didn't really test the things in which he was interested. This led to a large number (10 hours) of bug-fix stories to be applied to the third iteration that were just clarifications on existing stories.

In short, the acceptance tests were expensive to run, didn't really test what needed testing, and did not help us meet Lowell's expectations. It was past time to fix this.

This was the last iteration of the release. After this, the system would *really* go live. So, rather than add new features, Lowell scheduled all the new bug-fix stories and the story that integrated the new system into the existing Web site. Then he asked how we could fix the acceptance test problem.

We responded that we needed to investigate the technologies that would allow automated acceptance testing. The first technology we wanted to look at was httpunit. We felt that it would take us about three days to investigate it properly. So we proposed a three-day spike to Lowell. Lowell agreed.

Task planning was trivial because the bug-fix stories were equivalent to tasks. Two days were spent working on the tasks, and then the last three days of the iteration were spent looking into httpunit to see if it could be used as part of an acceptance testing framework.

The Failure to Create an Acceptance Testing Framework

The three days spent on this were interesting but did not turn out to be useful for this project. There were two reasons for this.

1. An acceptance test that used `httpunit` is written in Java. There was little hope that we could get Lowell to write Java code. To make an effective acceptance testing framework that included `httpunit`, we would have had to put some kind of convenient front end on it.

2. The urgency evaporated. Once the release was done, we had enough functionality to live with. It wasn't everything that we had originally planned, but it was enough. There were other priorities vying for our time, and Lowell directed the programmers away from this application.

If one or two more iterations had been scheduled; it seems likely that some kind of acceptance testing framework would have been created. It might simply have been a suite of Java programs that used `httpunit`, were written by the programmers, and were specified by Lowell. But as the momentum for the project waned, so did the need for the acceptance test framework.

Clearly, this is not an ideal situation. At some point the urgency on the registration system will heat up again, and we won't have automated acceptance tests. But it is what it is.

Release

The system went live as expected in early 2000, and it has been running without incident ever since. You can try it for yourself at *http:// www.objectmentor.com.*

The Release: Then and Now

At the end of Chapter 5, we showed the list of stories that Lowell had selected for the release. That list is duplicated here:

- ✧ User Story 4.6: *Login Story*
- ✧ User Story 4.7: *Cookies*
- ✧ User Story 4.8: *Guest Login*

- ✧ User Story 4.9: *Transparent Login*
- ✧ User Story 4.12: *Forgotten Password*
- ✧ User Story 4.15: *E-mail Notification*
- ✧ User Story 4.10: *User Registration*
- ✧ User Story 4.19: *Changing User Profile*
- ✧ User Story 4.13: *Migrate Access Data*
- ✧ User Story 4.5: *Smart Site Header*
- ✧ User Story 4.16: *Notification Specialization*

The release closed with the following stories in it:

- ✧ User Story 4.6: *Login Story*
- ✧ User Story 4.7: *Cookies*
- ✧ User Story 4.8: *Guest Login*
- ✧ User Story 4.9: *Transparent Login*
- ✧ User Story 4.12: *Forgotten Password*
- ✧ User Story 4.10: *User Registration*
- ✧ User Story 4.19: *Changing User Profile*
- ✧ User Story 4.16: *Notification Specialization*
- ✧ User Story 4.11: *Existing User*
- ✧ User Story 13.1: *Click for Overview*
- ✧ User Story 13.2: *Back with Filled Fields*
- ✧ User Story 13.3: *Registration Page Cosmetics*
- ✧ User Story 13.4: *Registration E-mail*
- ✧ User Story 13.5: *Combine Confirmation and Login*
- ✧ Some bug-fix stories from Iteration 3.

What a difference a few iterations can make. Now compare this with the initial prioritization from Chapter 5. We have reproduced the priority table in Table 14.2 and have boldfaced all completed stories. The stories in italics were really just constraints that helped to guide the implementation.

Notice that almost all the highest-priority stories were completed. Notice also that very few of the lower-priority tiers were completed. In fact, in the year since this release ended, these stories have never been implemented. Other priorities on other projects have taken precedence.

TABLE 14.2 Prioritized Stories from Table 5.1 (page 30)

Immediate	Short-term wait	Long-term wait
User Story 4.2: No Pop-Up Windows	User Story 4.1: Triggering the Login Mechanism	User Story 4.14: Legacy E-mail Addresses
User Story 4.3: Username as E-mail Address	User Story 4.5: Smart Site Header	**User Story 4.16:** Notification Specialization
User Story 4.6: Login Story	User Story 4.13: Migrate Access Data	User Story 4.17: Page Width
User Story 4.7: Cookies	**User Story 4.19:** Changing User Profile	User Story 4.18: Member Invitation
User Story 4.8: Guest Login		User Story 4.4: Porting Constraint
User Story 4.9: Transparent Login		
User Story 4.10: User Registration		
User Story 4.11: Existing User		
User Story 4.12: Forgotten Password		
User Story 4.15: E-mail Notification		

Indeed, it is not clear at this point whether these stories would be useful today.

Prioritizing by Technical Risk

The story with the highest technical risk in Table 5.1 was User Story 4.5: *Smart Site Header*. This story had a relatively high priority. We knew it wasn't needed in the first iteration, but it was scheduled for the release, so there was a strong feeling we'd need it very quickly. What if we had decided to prioritize our development based on the technical risk of this story? Implementing that story would have forced us to change *every* HTML Web page in the system! And all that work would have been for naught.

This is an interesting point. This story was considered a short-term need. It was scheduled for the first release. And yet, in the year that this application has been running, we haven't implemented, needed, or even missed it. What seems important at the beginning may not really be that important. The true priority of this story was discovered, and rediscovered, at each iteration planning meeting.

Clearly, Lowell had reason to delay the story. We made the estimate very high (five days, an entire iteration). It was high because there was a lot of uncertainty and work involved. This shows how the cost of a feature plays against its importance.

Still, the fact that the story was never implemented, either in the first three iterations or in the year since release shows that the initial prioritization was not long lived.

What If This Had Not Been an XP Project?

We would have started off by noting that we had three weeks of development time and about three weeks' worth of requirements. To save time we would have made the most sweeping changes first. User Story 4.5: *Smart Site Header* is, by far, the most sweeping of all the requirements; it touches everything and is essential infrastructure. So we would have done it first.

At the end of the three-week period, we would not have gotten the features that Lowell needed. We would have spent at least a third of our time on infrastructure that, in the end, would have provided no business value.

The project would probably have gone on for at least four weeks, and other important activities in other project areas would have been unnecessarily delayed.

Chapter 15

Conclusion

*I was amazed at the similarity between the problems
they had on their three-person project and the issues
we have on our sixty-person project.*

—Mike Two, Thoughtworks
(in a review of the early manuscript)

What can you learn from a three-week project? As it turns out, quite a bit. Clearly there's much more to learn from a project of larger scope. Still, this was a good first step at learning a new process. Having done this project, we were better prepared for bigger projects.

Projecting This Experience onto Larger Projects

In the year since we wrote this application, we have observed and participated in larger XP projects, here at Object Mentor and with our clients. The lessons we learned from this project have carried through to those others. Of the following three items, our simple project managed only to get the first right. We failed at the other two to some extent, and we felt the pain of that failure. We see similar failures, over and over again, as we are brought in to help struggling teams.

Short Cycles

The most important factor in any project is to divide it into small iterations. We've had many customers whose projects were completely stalled until they took that one simple bit of advice.

This is not simple advice to take. To divide a project into small iterations, you must ignore all the fears that come from not thinking the whole project through up front. Many teams are paralyzed by the fear that they might have to rework the initial code.

But in our experience, once they overcome that fear, they start to make progress. They build momentum and keep that momentum going.

What size iteration is best? For large projects, we like three weeks. For very small projects (less than two or three months), smaller iterations are more appropriate. The one-week iteration we chose for this book was appropriate for a three-week project.

Intense Communication

Just as important as small iterations is the need to communicate. When we walk into a customer site and see a bank of programmers all wearing headphones, with their monitors against the wall and their backs to each other,[1] we cringe. We want to see the developers working *together*. We want to see them pair programming or at least talking to each other on a frequent basis. We want them all to be working in the same room, and we want that room to have a healthy buzz of conversation. We don't believe that silence is the best environment for programming. (Neither do those who wear headphones.)

We often find ourselves helping engineering teams who have difficulty getting requirements. These teams don't seem to be able to talk to the business or marketing folks. There are many reasons for this. Often the marketing folks are out doing defensive sales and don't have time to work with the engineers.

This is a disaster. We want to see the developers and business folks communicating on a regular basis. We want to see business decisions made by business people and technical decisions made by technical people.

---

1. I saw an advertisement in a train station that was an attempt to recruit software people for a growing company. It said something to the effect of: "Come here and rub cerebellums with the best software minds in the world." This failed attempt at erudition was ironic. I think the advertiser probably meant to use the term *cerebrum*, the thinking part of the brain. The cerebellum is the section of the brain that regulates fine motor activity. It is positioned at the very back of the brain. To rub cerebellums, two people must have their backs to each other.

Feedback

One of the most glaring symptoms of a dysfunctional team is the production of vast amounts of artifacts or code without any verification that what they are producing is relevant to their project. We have seen teams get paralyzed in the production of vast use-case documents or huge design models. We've also seen piles of infrastructure code written long before anyone might use it.[2]

Even when the technical issues are under control, we have frequently seen a lack of feedback from the business and customer. We've seen beautifully crafted projects that utterly failed to meet the needs of the business.

When we visit a client, we like to see feedback mechanisms in place for all artifacts. We want that feedback to be rapid, intense, and honest.

Lessons Learned

Following are the lessons that we have learned in this project, and in the many other XP projects we've worked on since.

- ◇ **Test the hard stuff.** We thought testing servlets was too hard, so we didn't do it. This turned out to bite us later (see *We Didn't Write Tests* on page 65).
- ◇ **Make sure customer writes acceptance tests.** Lowell did not write the acceptance tests for our project. Thus, at the end of each iteration, he was surprised by some of the functionality and wrote stories to correct it. This story thrashing could have been minimized if he had written the acceptance tests (see Chapter 14).
- ◇ **Reduce dependencies when you test.** In order to test modules in isolation, use spoof interfaces (see *Spoofing* on page 92).
- ◇ **Stick to your guns.** During the first iteration plan, we allowed Lowell to convince us that we could do a little more than we estimated. This caused us to do less refactoring than we should have done (see page 44).

---

2. We've written some of that—but that was a long time ago.

◇ **Change plans only when you have a story and an estimate.** A long and painful misunderstanding could have been prevented simply by sticking to the process rather than trying to shortcut it (see *An Interesting Misunderstanding* on page 130).

◇ **Even small projects need a process.** The reason we did this project was because our previous implementation was done without a process and failed (see Chapter 1).

◇ **Keep process light.** Just because you need a process doesn't mean you need a huge process. We like to use the least amount of process we can get away with (see Chapter 2).

◇ **Story writing is chaotic.** We found that stories were not written in a nice, orderly fashion. The partial writing of one leads to the partial writing of another and the correction of the first. The stories intertwine and evolve concurrently (see Chapter 4).

◇ **Don't anticipate infrastructure.** We got ourselves into a bit of trouble by anticipating infrastructure even in this small project. (See *Infrastructure* on page 48. Also see Chapter 11.)

◇ **Tests eliminate fear of change.** The part of our code that was heavily covered by unit tests was very easy to change because we weren't afraid we would break anything (see the *Conclusion* in Chapter 7).

◇ **Manual tests slow you down and make you take larger steps.** Because the manual tests were hard to run, we found we ran them a lot less often. This meant we did more work between tests and did less refactoring (see Chapter 9).

◇ **Back into solutions from initial premises.** This is a very intriguing form of development (see Chapter 10).

◇ **Drive functionality out of things that are hard to test.** Any module that is hard to test will be hard to refactor. So drive as much functionality out of those modules as possible (see the *Conclusion* in Chapter 11).

◇ **Early infrastructure creates a false sense of security.** We built the database infrastructure first. This made us feel that we had accomplished something. Later, when we actually used it, we had to rewrite it (see Chapter 11).

Final Conclusions

How well did we do XP? In hindsight, we give the project a rousing C++ for process conformance.[3] We struggled with tests first and opted not to test things we later realized we should have tested. We allowed our customer to talk us into adding an extra 25% to the first iteration. We anticipated infrastructure. We fell off process in a crisis. We didn't actively pursue our customer when communications broke down. We had no opportunity to do continuous integration.

But we did do a lot of things right. All production code was written in pairs. We did lots of testing, mostly up front. We used short cycles with lots of feedback. We had the customer drive priorities. We worked through the communications issues with our customer. And—we delivered.

XP worked for us. This isn't a big surprise. It's fairly difficult to fail when doing a three-week project. Also, we've successfully used various agile processes for over a decade, so XP wasn't *that* different from what we were used to.

Perhaps it seems unreasonable to draw conclusions from a three-week, two- to three-person project. Certainly it would be silly to use our experience from this project to justify a full transition of a multi-person-century project to XP. However, this tiny project involved many of the problems that arise in larger projects. We believe that the solutions XP brought to the problems we encountered can be reasonably extended to larger projects.

---

3. Retch—what a horrible term.

Appendix

Iteration 1—Source Code

LISTING A.1 AllDatabaseTests.java

```java
import junit.framework.*;

public class AllDatabaseTests
{
  public static void main(String[] args)
  {
    junit.textui.TestRunner.run(suite());
  }

  public static Test suite()
  {
    TestSuite suite=new TestSuite("All Database Tests");
    suite.addTest(UserTest.suite());
    suite.addTest(DatabaseAccessTest.suite());
    suite.addTest(DatabaseConnectionTest.suite());
    suite.addTest(DatabaseAddTest.suite());
    suite.addTest(DatabaseStaticTest.suite());
    suite.addTest(ForgotPasswordTest.suite());
    suite.addTest(EmailTest.suite());
    return suite;
  }
}
```

```java
import java.sql.*;

class Database
{
  static
  {
    try
    {
      Class.forName("sun.jdbc.odbc.JdbcOdbcDriver");
    }
    catch(ClassNotFoundException e)
    {
      e.printStackTrace();
      System.exit(1);
    }
  }

  public Database(String ds)
  {
    dataSource=ds;
  }

  public void open() throws SQLException
  {
    con=DriverManager.getConnection("jdbc:odbc:"
                                    +dataSource,"","");
  }

  public boolean isOpen() throws SQLException
  {
    return !con.isClosed();
  }

  public void close() throws SQLException
  {
    if(con!=null)
      con.close();
  }

  public User findUserByEmail(String emailAddress)
  {
    User user=null;
    try
    {
```

```java
        Statement statement=con.createStatement();
        ResultSet rs=statement.executeQuery(
          "SELECT * FROM userlist WHERE emailAddress = '"
          +emailAddress+"'");
        boolean found=false;
        while(rs.next()&&!found){
          found=true;
          user=new User(rs.getString("emailAddress"),
                        rs.getString("password"),
                        rs.getString("firstName"),
                        rs.getString("lastName"),
                        rs.getString("organization"),
                        rs.getBoolean("notification"));
        }
        rs.close();
      }
      catch(SQLException e){}
      return user;
    }

    public boolean addUser(User u)
    {
      try
      {
        Statement statement=con.createStatement();
        statement
          .executeUpdate("INSERT INTO userlist VALUES "+"('"
                        +u.getEmailAddress()+"','"
                        +u.getPassword()+"','"
                        +u.getOrganization()+"','"
                        +u.getFirstName()+"','"
                        +u.getLastName()+"',"
                        +u.getNotification()+")");
      }
      catch(Exception e)
      {
        return false;
      }
      return true;
    }

    public boolean deleteUser(String emailAddress)
    {
      boolean result=false;
```

Listing continued on next page.

```
    try
    {
      Statement statement=con.createStatement();
      statement.executeUpdate(
        "DELETE FROM userlist WHERE emailAddress = '"
        +emailAddress+"'");
      result=true;
    }
    catch(SQLException e)
    {
      result=false;
    }
    return result;
  }

  private Connection con;
  private String dataSource;
}
```

LISTING A.3 DatabaseAccessTest.java

```
import junit.framework.*;

public class DatabaseAccessTest extends TestCase
{
  private Database db;
  public DatabaseAccessTest(String name)
  {
    super(name);
  }

  public static Test suite()
  {
    return new TestSuite(DatabaseAccessTest.class);
  }

  protected void setUp() throws Exception
  {
    db=new Database("websiteusers");
    db.open();
  }
```

LISTING A.3 DatabaseAccessTest.java (*continued*)

```java
  protected void tearDown() throws Exception
  {
    db.close();
  }

  public void testNotFound() throws Exception
  {
    User u=db.findUserByEmail("noname@badvalue.com");
    assert(u==null);
  }

  public void testNull() throws Exception
  {
    User u=db.findUserByEmail(null);
    assert(u==null);
  }

  public void testZeroLengthEmail() throws Exception
  {
    User u=db.findUserByEmail("");
    assert(u==null);
  }

  public void testRead() throws Exception
  {
    User u=db.findUserByEmail("newkirk@objectmentor.com");
    assert(u!=null);
    assertEquals("newkirk@objectmentor.com",
                 u.getEmailAddress());
    assertEquals("jim",u.getPassword());
    assertEquals("James",u.getFirstName());
    assertEquals("Newkirk",u.getLastName());
    assertEquals("Object Mentor, Inc.",
                 u.getOrganization());
    assert(u.getNotification());
  }

  public void testLogin() throws Exception
  {
    User u=db.findUserByEmail("bbutton@objectmentor.com");
    assert(u.validate("brian"));
  }
}
```

LISTING A.4 DatabaseAddTest.java

```java
import junit.framework.*;

public class DatabaseAddTest extends TestCase
{
  private Database db;
  private User user1;
  private String email1="123@universe.com";

  public DatabaseAddTest(String name)
  {
    super(name);
  }

  public static Test suite()
  {
    return new TestSuite(DatabaseAddTest.class);
  }

  protected void setUp() throws Exception
  {
    user1=new User(email1,"456","First","Last",
                   "The Universe",false);
    db=new Database("websiteusers");
    db.open();
  }

  protected void tearDown() throws Exception
  {
    db.close();
  }

  public void testAdd() throws Exception
  {
    assert(db.findUserByEmail(email1)==null);
    assert(db.addUser(user1)==true);
    User dbUser=db.findUserByEmail(email1);
    assert(dbUser!=null);
    assertEquals(user1,dbUser);
    db.deleteUser(email1);
    assert(db.findUserByEmail(email1)==null);
  }

  public void testDuplicate() throws Exception
  {
```

LISTING A.4 DatabaseAddTest.java (*continued*)

```java
      assert(db.findUserByEmail(email1)==null);
      assert(db.addUser(user1)==true);
      assert(db.addUser(user1)==false);
      db.deleteUser(email1);
      assert(db.findUserByEmail(email1)==null);
    }
  }
```

LISTING A.5 DatabaseConnectionTest.java

```java
import junit.framework.*;
import java.sql.*;

public class DatabaseConnectionTest extends TestCase
{
  public DatabaseConnectionTest(String name)
  {
    super(name);
  }

  public static Test suite()
  {
    return new TestSuite(DatabaseConnectionTest.class);
  }

  public void testConnect() throws Throwable
  {
    Database db=new Database("websiteusers");
    db.open();
    assert(db.isOpen());
    db.close();
    assert(!db.isOpen());
  }

  // this was added due to a bug
  public void testClose() throws Throwable
  {
    Database db=new Database("websiteusers");
    db.close();
  }
}
```

LISTING A.6 DatabaseStaticTest.java

```java
import junit.framework.*;

public class DatabaseStaticTest extends TestCase
{
  private User user1;
  private String email1="123@universe.com";

  public DatabaseStaticTest(String name)
  {
    super(name);
  }

  public static Test suite()
  {
    return new TestSuite(DatabaseStaticTest.class);
  }

  protected void setUp() throws Exception
  {
    user1=new User(email1,"456","First","Last",
                   "The Universe",false);
  }

  public void testAdd() throws Exception
  {
    assert(UserDatabase.findUser(email1)==null);
    assert(UserDatabase.add(user1)==true);
    User dbUser=UserDatabase.findUser(email1);
    assert(dbUser!=null);
    assertEquals(user1,dbUser);
    assert(UserDatabase.delete(email1));
    assert(UserDatabase.findUser(email1)==null);
  }

  public void testDuplicate() throws Exception
  {
    assert(UserDatabase.findUser(email1)==null);
    assert(UserDatabase.add(user1)==true);
    assert(UserDatabase.add(user1)==false);
    assert(UserDatabase.delete(email1));
    assert(UserDatabase.findUser(email1)==null);
  }

  public void testValidateLogin() throws Exception
  {
```

```java
    assert(UserDatabase
      .validateLogin("newkirk@objectmentor.com","jim"));
    assert(!UserDatabase
      .validateLogin("123@objectmentor.com","test"));
    assert(!UserDatabase.validateLogin("","test"));
    assert(!UserDatabase
      .validateLogin("newkirk@objectmentor.com","test"));
    assert(!UserDatabase.validateLogin(null,null));
  }

  public void testPasswordNotFound()
  {
    assert(UserDatabase.findPasswordFromEmail("notFound")
        ==null);
  }

  public void testPasswordFound()
  {
    assertEquals("jim",UserDatabase
      .findPasswordFromEmail("newkirk@objectmentor.com"));
  }

  public void testPasswordNull()
  {
    assert(UserDatabase.findPasswordFromEmail(null)==null);
  }
}
```

LISTING A.7 EmailTest.java

```java
import junit.framework.*;

public class EmailTest extends TestCase
{
  public EmailTest(String name)
  {
    super(name);
  }

  public static Test suite()
  {
    return new TestSuite(EmailTest.class);
  }
```

Listing continued on next page.

```java
    public void testBadEmailAddr()
    {
      Mailer m=new SMTPMailer("mail.wwa.com");
      assert(m.send("noAt","subj","body")==false);
    }

    public void testBadMailHost()
    {
      Mailer m=new SMTPMailer("wwa.com");
      assert(m.send("newkirk@objectmentor.com","subj","body")
             ==false);
    }

    public void testSuccess()
    {
      Mailer m=new SMTPMailer("mail.wwa.com");
      assert(m.send("newkirk@objectmentor.com","subj","body")
             ==true);
    }
  }
```

LISTING A.8 ForgotPasswordTest.java

```java
import junit.framework.*;

public class ForgotPasswordTest extends TestCase
{
  public ForgotPasswordTest(String name)
  {
    super(name);
  }

  public static Test suite()
  {
    return new TestSuite(ForgotPasswordTest.class);
  }

  private boolean mailSent;
  private String theToAddr;
  private String theSubj;
  private String theBody;

  public void setup()
  {
    mailSent=false;
    theToAddr="";
```

```
      theSubj="";
      theBody="";
    }

    public void testNoUser()
    {
      String noUser="IDon'tExist";
      PasswordReminderDatabase db=
        new PasswordReminderDatabase()
      {
        public String findPasswordFromEmail(String email)
        {
          return null;
        }
      };
      Mailer m=new Mailer()
      {
        public boolean send(String to,String subject,
                            String body)
        {
          mailSent=true;
          return true;
        }
      };
      PasswordReminder pr=new PasswordReminder(db,m);
      assert(pr.remind(noUser)
             ==PasswordReminder.NOEMAILFOUND);
      assert(mailSent==false);
    }  // testNoUser

    public void testBadEmail()
    {
      PasswordReminderDatabase db=
        new PasswordReminderDatabase()
      {
        public String findPasswordFromEmail(String email)
        {
          return "saba";
        }
      };
      Mailer m=new Mailer()
      {
        public boolean send(String to,String subj,
                            String body)
```

Listing continued on next page.

```
          {
            theToAddr=to;
            theSubj=subj;
            theBody=body;
            return false;
          }
      };
      PasswordReminder pr=new PasswordReminder(db,m);
      assertEquals(PasswordReminder.EMAILERROR,
                       pr.remind("Bob"));
      assertEquals("Bob",theToAddr);
      assertEquals("Your Object Mentor Password",theSubj);
      assertEquals("Your Object Mentor Password is saba",
                       theBody);
  }  // testBadEmail

  public void testGoodEmail()
  {
      PasswordReminderDatabase db=
        new PasswordReminderDatabase()
      {
        public String findPasswordFromEmail(String email)
        {
          return "saba";
        }
      };
      Mailer m=new Mailer()
      {
        public boolean send(String to,String subj,
                             String body)
        {
          theToAddr=to;
          theSubj=subj;
          theBody=body;
          return true;
        }
      };
      PasswordReminder pr=new PasswordReminder(db,m);
      assertEquals(PasswordReminder.OK,pr.remind("Bob"));
      assertEquals("Bob",theToAddr);
      assertEquals("Your Object Mentor Password",theSubj);
      assertEquals("Your Object Mentor Password is saba",
                       theBody);
  }  // testGoodEmail
}  // ForgotPasswordTest
```

LISTING A.9 `Mailer.java`

```java
public interface Mailer
{
  public boolean send(String to,String subj,String body);
}
```

LISTING A.10 `PasswordDatabaseAdapter.java`

```java
public class PasswordDatabaseAdapter
        implements PasswordReminderDatabase
{
  public String findPasswordFromEmail(String email)
  {
    return UserDatabase.findPasswordFromEmail(email);
  }
}
```

LISTING A.11 `PasswordReminder.java`

```java
public class PasswordReminder
{
  public static final int OK=0;
  public static final int NOEMAILFOUND=1;
  public static final int EMAILERROR=2;

  private PasswordReminderDatabase itsDb;
  private Mailer itsMailer;

  public PasswordReminder(PasswordReminderDatabase db,
                          Mailer m)
  {
    itsDb=db;
    itsMailer=m;
  }

  public int remind(String email)
  {
    int status=OK;
```

Listing continued on next page.

```
      String password=itsDb.findPasswordFromEmail(email);
      if(password!=null){
        boolean wasSent=
          itsMailer.send(email,"Your Object Mentor Password",
                         "Your Object Mentor Password is "
                         +password);
        if(!wasSent)
          status=EMAILERROR;
      }
      else
        status=NOEMAILFOUND;
      return status;
    }
}
```

LISTING A.12 `PasswordReminderDatabase.java`

```
public interface PasswordReminderDatabase
{
  public String findPasswordFromEmail(String email);
}
```

LISTING A.13 `SMTPMailer.java`

```
import java.io.*;
import com.oreilly.servlet.MailMessage;

public class SMTPMailer implements Mailer
{
  private String mailHost;

  public SMTPMailer(String mailHost)
  {
    this.mailHost=mailHost;
  }

  public boolean send(String to,String subj,String body)
  {
    boolean sent=true;
    try
    {
      MailMessage msg=new MailMessage(mailHost);
      msg.from("info@objectmentor.com");
```

```
      msg.to(to);
      msg.setSubject(subj);
      PrintStream out=msg.getPrintStream();
      out.println(body);
      msg.sendAndClose();
    }
    catch(IOException e)
    {
      e.printStackTrace();
      sent=false;
    }
    return sent;
  }
}
```

LISTING A.14 User.java

```
public class User
{
  private String email;
  private String firstName;
  private String lastName;
  private String password;
  private boolean notification;
  private String organization;

  public User(String email,String password,
              String firstName,String lastName,
              String organization,boolean notify)
  {
    this.email=email;
    this.password=password;
    this.firstName=firstName;
    this.lastName=lastName;
    this.notification=notify;
    this.organization=organization;
  }

  public String getEmailAddress()
  {
    return email;
  }
```

Listing continued on next page.

```java
public String getFirstName()
{
  return firstName;
}

public String getLastName()
{
  return lastName;
}

public String getPassword()
{
  return password;
}

public boolean getNotification()
{
  return notification;
}

public boolean validate(String password)
{
  return (this.password.equals(password));
}

public String getOrganization()
{
  return organization;
}

public boolean equals(Object o)
{
  if(o==this)
    return true;
  if(o==null)
    return false;
  if(o instanceof User){
    User rhs=(User)o;
    return ((email
      .equals(rhs.getEmailAddress()))&&(password
      .equals(rhs.getPassword()))&&(organization
      .equals(rhs.getOrganization()))&&(firstName
      .equals(rhs.getFirstName()))&&(lastName
```

```
          .equals(rhs.getLastName()))&&(notification==rhs
          .getNotification()));
      }
      return false;
    }
  }
```

LISTING A.15 UserDatabase.java

```java
import java.sql.*;

public class UserDatabase
{
  public static Database open() throws Error
  {
    Database db=null;
    try
    {
      db=new Database("websiteusers");
      db.open();
    }
    catch(SQLException e)
    {
      throw new Error(e.toString());
    }
    return db;
  }

  public static void close(Database db) throws Error
  {
    try
    {
      if(db!=null)
        db.close();
    }
    catch(SQLException e)
    {
      throw new Error(e.toString());
    }
  }
```

Listing continued on next page.

```java
  public static String findPasswordFromEmail(String email)
  {
    String result=null;
    User u=findUser(email);
    if(u!=null)
      result=u.getPassword();
    return result;
  }

  public static User findUser(String email) throws Error
  {
    Database db=open();
    User result=db.findUserByEmail(email);
    close(db);
    return result;
  }

  public static boolean validateLogin(String email,
                                      String password)
  {
    boolean result=false;
    Database db=open();
    User u=db.findUserByEmail(email);
    if(u!=null)
      result=u.validate(password);
    close(db);
    return result;
  }

  public static boolean add(User newUser) throws Error
  {
    Database db=open();
    boolean result=db.addUser(newUser);
    close(db);
    return result;
  }

  public static boolean delete(String email) throws Error
  {
    Database db=open();
    boolean result=db.deleteUser(email);
    close(db);
    return result;
  }
}
```

LISTING A.16 UserTest.java

```java
import junit.framework.*;

public class UserTest extends TestCase
{
  public UserTest(String name)
  {
    super(name);
  }

  public static Test suite()
  {
    return new TestSuite(UserTest.class);
  }

  public void testCreate()
  {
    User c=new User("newkirk@objectmentor.com","password",
                    "James","Newkirk",
                    "Object Mentor, Inc.",true);
    assertEquals("newkirk@objectmentor.com",
                 c.getEmailAddress());
    assertEquals("password",c.getPassword());
    assertEquals("James",c.getFirstName());
    assertEquals("Newkirk",c.getLastName());
    assertEquals("Object Mentor, Inc.",
                 c.getOrganization());
    assert(c.validate("password"));
    assert(!c.validate("jim"));
    assert(c.getNotification());
  }

  public void testEquals()
  {
    User c1=new User("button@objectmentor.com","brian",
                    "Brian","Button",
                    "Object Mentor, Inc.",false);
    User c2=new User("newkirk@objectmentor.com","password",
                    "James","Newkirk",
                    "Object Mentor, Inc.",true);
    User c3=new User("button@objectmentor.com","brian",
                    "Brian","Button",
                    "Object Mentor, Inc.",false);
    assert(!c1.equals(c2));
    assert(c1.equals(c3));
```

Listing continued on next page.

```
      assert(!c1.equals(null));
      assert(!c1.equals(new String("")));
      assert(c1.equals(c1));
   }
}
```

LISTING A.17 CheckForLogin.java

```
import java.io.*;

import javax.servlet.*;
import javax.servlet.http.*;

public class CheckForLogin extends HttpServlet
{
  public void service(
          HttpServletRequest request,
          HttpServletResponse response)
              throws ServletException,IOException
  {
    HttpSession s=request.getSession(true);
    if(!sessionInProgress(s)
           &&!cookieIsValid(request.getCookies()))
      doLogin(request,response);
  }

  private void doLogin(
          HttpServletRequest request,
          HttpServletResponse response)
              throws ServletException,IOException
  {
    response.sendRedirect("/userproject/register.jsp?url="
                            +request.getRequestURI());
  }

  private boolean sessionInProgress(HttpSession session)
  {
    boolean inProgress=false;
    String name=(String)session.getValue("email");
    if(name!=null&&name.length()>0)
      inProgress=true;
    return inProgress;
  }
```

LISTING A.17 CheckForLogin.java *(continued)*

```java
  private boolean cookieIsValid(Cookie[] cookies)
  {
    boolean valid=false;
    boolean found=false;
    if(cookies!=null){
      for(int i=0;i<cookies.length&&!found;i++){
        Cookie c=cookies[i];
        if(c!=null){
          String name=c.getName();
          String value=c.getValue();
          System.out.println("Cookies: "+name+", value:"
                             +value);
          if(name!=null){
            if(name.equals("email")){
              found=true;
              System.out.println("email cookie found");
              if(value!=null&&value.length()>0){
                valid=true;
              }
            }  // name == email
          }    // name != null
        }        // cookie != null
      }          // for
    }            // cookies != null
    return valid;
  }  // cookieIsvalid
}
```

LISTING A.18 bademailaddress.jsp

```jsp
<head>
<title>password sent page</title>
<%@ include file="header.jsp" %>
<tr>
<td align="right" width="255" height="34"> </td>
<td bgcolor="#008080" width="4" height="34"> </td>
<td height="1" width="275">
<table cellpadding="3">
<tr>
<td><font face="arial, helvetica" size="2">
<b>There was a problem sending to:
<%= request.getParameter("email") %>
```

Listing continued on next page.

LISTING A.18 `bademailaddress.jsp` *(continued)*

```
</b>.
</font><font face="arial, helvetica" size="2">
<p>
<a href='/userproject/fpassword.jsp?url=
<%= request.getParameter("url")%>'>
<b>Click here to try again! </b></a>
</p>
</font></td>
</tr>
</table>
</td>
</tr>
<%@ include file="row-space.jsp" %></TBODY></TABLE></BODY>
</head>

</html>
```

LISTING A.19 `default.html`

```
<html>

<head>
<meta http-equiv="Content-Type" content="text/html;
charset=windows-1252">
<meta name="GENERATOR" content="Microsoft FrontPage 4.0">
<meta name="ProgId" content="FrontPage.Editor.Document">
<title>New Page 1</title>
</head>

<body>

<p><a href="/userproject/protectedPage.shtml">
          Protected Page</a></p>

<p> </p>

<p><a href="http://127.0.0.1/servlet/ResetServlet">
          Reset</a></p>

</body>

</html>
```

```java
import java.io.*;

import javax.servlet.*;
import javax.servlet.http.*;

public class ForgotPassword extends HttpServlet
{
  private HttpServletRequest request;
  private HttpServletResponse response;
  private String email;
  private String url;
  public void doGet(
          HttpServletRequest req,HttpServletResponse resp)
            throws ServletException,IOException
  {
    request=req;
    response=resp;
    email=(String)request.getParameter("email");
    url=(String)request.getParameter("url");
    PasswordReminderDatabase db=
      new PasswordDatabaseAdapter();
    Mailer m=
      new SMTPMailer(getInitParameter("mail-server"));
    PasswordReminder pr=new PasswordReminder(db,m);
    int status=pr.remind(email);
    if(status==PasswordReminder.OK)
      redirect("sent");
    else
      if(status==PasswordReminder.EMAILERROR)
        redirect("bademail");
      else
        if(status==PasswordReminder.NOEMAILFOUND)
          redirect("noemail");
  }

  private void redirect(String base)
          throws ServletException,IOException
  {
    String baseURI=getInitParameter(base);
    String uri=baseURI+"?email="+email+"&url="+url;
    response.sendRedirect(uri);
  }
```

Listing continued on next page.

LISTING A.20 ForgotPassword.java *(continued)*

```java
    public void doPost(
            HttpServletRequest request,HttpServletResponse
                response)
                throws ServletException,IOException
    {
      doGet(request,response);
    }
  }
```

LISTING A.21 fpassword.jsp

```html
<HTML>
<HEAD>
<TITLE>
xpinpractice.com forgot password page
</TITLE>

<%@ include file="header.jsp" %>

<form method="POST" action="/servlet/forgotpassword">
<TR>
<TD align=right width="255" height="34"> 
</TD>
<TD bgColor=#008080 width=4 height="34"> 
</TD>
<TD height="1" width="275">
<font face="arial, helvetica" size="2">
<b>
  Email password
</b>
</font>
</TD>
</TR>
<%@ include file="row-space.jsp" %>
<TR>
<TD align=right width="255" height="34">
<p align="right">
<font face="arial, helvetica" size="2">
<b>
Email address   
</b>
</font>
</p>
```

```
</TD>
<TD bgColor=#008080 width=4 height="10">
<IMG border=0 height=1 src="images/spacer.gif" width=1>
</TD>
<TD height="34" width="275">
<FONT face="arial, helvetica" size=3> 
<input type="text" name="email" size="30">
</FONT>
<IMG border=0 height=1 src="images/spacer.gif" width=1>
</TD>
</TR>
<%@ include file="row-space.jsp" %>
<TR>
<TD align=right width="255" height="34">
<p align="right">
<font face="arial, helvetica" size="2">
<b>
That's all . . .   
</b>
</font>
</p>
</TD>
<TD bgColor=#008080 width=4 height="34">
<IMG border=0 height=1 src="images/spacer.gif" width=1>
</TD>
<TD height="27" width="275">
<FONT face="arial, helvetica" size=3> </FONT>
<IMG border=0 height=1 src="images/spacer.gif" width=1>
<input type="submit" value="Send password" name="Send
               password">
</TD>
</TR>
<input type=hidden name="url" value="<%=
                        request.getParameter("url") %>">
</FORM>
<%@ include file="row-space.jsp" %>
</TBODY>
</TABLE>

</BODY>
</HTML>
```

LISTING A.22 GuestServlet.java

```java
import java.io.*;
import javax.servlet.*;
import javax.servlet.http.*;

public class GuestServlet extends RedirectingServlet
{
  public void execute()
    throws ServletException, IOException
  {
    saveUserInSession("guest");
  }
}
```

LISTING A.23 header.jsp

```html
<BODY leftMargin=5 link=#000066 topMargin=5 vLink=#006699
marginheight="5" marginwidth="5">
<CENTER>

<TABLE border=0 cellPadding=0 cellSpacing=0 width=540
height="93">
<TBODY>

<TR>
<TD align=center height="200" width="538" colspan="3">
<p align="center">
<img border="0" src="images/XPPracWeb.jpg"
width="300" height="189" align="left">
</p>
</TD>
</CENTER>
</TR>
<TR>
<TD align=right height="15" bgcolor="#008080"
width="538" colspan="3">
<p align="center">
<b>
<A href="http://www.xpinpractice.com">
<FONT color=#FFFFFF face="arial, helvetica"
size=2>click for additional information</FONT>
</A>
```

LISTING A.23 header.jsp (*continued*)

```
<FONT color=#FFFFFF face="arial, helvetica"
size=2> or call 1-800-338-6716 </FONT>
</b>
</p>
</TD>
</TR>
```

LISTING A.24 login.jsp

```
<HTML>
<HEAD>
<TITLE>
XP in Practice.com Login
</TITLE>

<%
String email = request.getParameter("email");
if(email == null)
email = "";
%>

<%@ include file="header.jsp" %>

<FORM method="POST" action="/servlet/login">
<TR>
<TD align=right width=255 height="34">
<font face="arial, helvetica" size="2">
<b>
E-mail address   
</b>
</font>
</TD>
<TD bgColor=#008080 width=4 height="34">
<IMG border=0 height=1 src="images/spacer.gif" width=1>
</TD>
<TD height="1" width="275">
<IMG border=0 height=1 src="images/spacer.gif" width=2>
<FONT face="arial, helvetica" size=3>
<INPUT type=text maxLength=100 name="emailAddress" size="30"
value="<%=email%>"
```

Listing continued on next page.

```
></FONT>
</TD>
</TR>
<%@ include file="row-space.jsp" %>
<TR>
<TD align=right width=255 height="34">
<font face="arial, helvetica" size="2">
<b>
Password   
</b>
</font>
</TD>
<TD bgColor=#008080 width=4 height="25">
 
</TD>
<TD height="25" width="275">
<IMG border=0 height=1 src="images/spacer.gif" width=2>
<FONT face="arial, helvetica" size=3>
<INPUT maxLength="30" name="password" size="15"
type="password">
</FONT>
</TD>
</TR>
<%@ include file="row-space.jsp" %>
<TR>
<TD align=right width=255 height="34">
<font face="arial, helvetica" size="2">
<b>
Remember password   
</b>
</font>
</TD>
<TD bgColor=#008080 width=4 height="34">
<IMG border=0 height=1 src="images/spacer.gif" width=1>
</TD>
<TD height="34" width="275">
<FONT face="arial, helvetica" size=3> 
<INPUT CHECKED name=remember type="checkbox" value="true">
</FONT>
</TD>
</TR>
<%@ include file="row-space.jsp" %>
<TR>
<TD align=right width=255 height="34">
<font face="arial, helvetica" size="2">
```

```
<b>
That's all . . .   
</b>
</font>
</TD>
<TD bgColor=#008080 width=4 height="34">
<IMG border=0 height=1 src="images/spacer.gif" width=1>
</TD>
<TD height="27" width="275">
<IMG border=0 height=1 src="images/spacer.gif" width=2>
<FONT face="arial, helvetica" size=3>
<INPUT name=login type=submit value="  log in  ">
</FONT>
</TD>
</TR>
<%@ include file="row-space.jsp" %>
<input type=hidden name="url" value="<%=
request.getParameter("url") %>">
</FORM>
<TR>
<TD align=right width=255 height="34">
<font face="arial, helvetica" size="2">
<b>
Forgot your password?  
</b>
</font>
</TD>
<TD bgColor=#008080 width=4 height="34">
<IMG border=0 height=1 src="images/spacer.gif" width=1>
</TD>
<TD height="34" width="275">
<IMG border=0 height=1 src="images/spacer.gif" width=2>
<FONT face="arial, helvetica" size=3>
<A href="/userproject/fpassword.jsp?url=<%=
request.getParameter("url") %>">
Email me!
</A>
</FONT>
</TD>
</TR>
<%@ include file="row-space.jsp" %>
</TBODY>
</TABLE>
</BODY>
</HTML>
```

LISTING A.25 LoginServlet.java

```java
import java.io.*;

import javax.servlet.*;
import javax.servlet.http.HttpServlet;
import javax.servlet.http.HttpServletRequest;
import javax.servlet.http.HttpServletResponse;
import javax.servlet.http.HttpSession;
import javax.servlet.http.Cookie;

public class LoginServlet extends RedirectingServlet
{
  private String itsUserId;
  public void execute()
          throws ServletException,IOException
  {
    itsUserId=itsRequest.getParameter("emailAddress");
    String password=itsRequest.getParameter("password");
    if(UserDatabase.validateLogin(itsUserId,password)){
      saveUserInSession(itsUserId);
      if(shouldWriteCookie())
        saveUserInCookie();
    }
  }

  private boolean shouldWriteCookie()
  {
    boolean writeCookie=true;
    String stringRem=itsRequest.getParameter("remember");
    if(stringRem==null)
      writeCookie=false;
    return writeCookie;
  }

  private void saveUserInCookie()
  {
    Cookie cookie=new Cookie("email",itsUserId);
    cookie.setMaxAge(86400*365);  // 1 year approximatly
    cookie.setPath("/");
    itsResponse.addCookie(cookie);
  }
}
```

LISTING A.26 `noemailfound.jsp`

```html
<HTML>
<HEAD>
<TITLE>
no email found error page
</TITLE>

<%@ include file="header.jsp" %>

<TR>
<TD align=right width="255" height="34"> 
</TD>
<TD bgColor=#008080 width=4 height="34"> 
</TD>
<TD height="1" width="275">
<TABLE cellpadding="3">
<TR>
<TD>
<font face="arial, helvetica" size="2">
<b>
The e-mail address: <%= request.getParameter("email") %>
is not in our database.
</b>
</font>
<font face="arial, helvetica, ms sans serif" size=2>
<p>
<a href="/userproject/fpassword.jsp?url=<%=
request.getParameter("url") %>">
<b>
Click here to try again!
</b>
</a>
</p>
</font>
<font face="arial, helvetica, ms sans serif" size=2>
<p>
<a href="/userproject/register.jsp?url=<%=
request.getParameter("url") %>">
<b>
Click here to register.
</b>
```

Listing continued on next page.

LISTING A.26 noemailfound.jsp *(continued)*

```
</a>
</p>
</font>
</TD>
</TR>
</TABLE>
</TD>
</TR>
<%@ include file="row-space.jsp" %>
</TBODY>
</TABLE>

</BODY>
</HTML>
```

LISTING A.27 PasswordGenerator.java

```java
public class PasswordGenerator
{
  public static String generatePassword()
  {
    StringBuffer password=new StringBuffer();
    for(int i=0;i<8;i++)
      password.append(generateRandomCharacter());
    return new String(password);
  }

  private static char generateRandomCharacter()
  {
    double x=Math.random();
    x*=26;
    return (char)('a'+x);
  }
}
```

LISTING A.28 `passwordsent.jsp`

```
<HTML>
<HEAD>
<TITLE>
password sent page
</TITLE>
<%@ include file="header.jsp" %>

<TR>
<TD align=right width="255" height="34"> 
</TD>
<TD bgColor=#008080 width=4 height="34"> 
</TD>
<TD height="1" width="275">
<TABLE cellpadding="3">
<TR>
<TD>
<font face="arial, helvetica" size="2">
<b>
A mail has been sent to your email address to remind you of
your password.
</b>
</font>
<font face="arial, helvetica, ms sans serif" size=2>
<p>
Click
<a href="/userproject/login.jsp?url
=<%=request.getParameter("url")%>&email
=<%=request.getParameter("email")%>">
<b>here</b></a>
to login!
</p>
</font>
</TD>
</TR>
</TABLE>
</TD>
</TR>
<%@ include file="row-space.jsp" %>
</TBODY>
</TABLE>

</BODY>
</HTML>
```

LISTING A.29 `RedirectingServlet.java`

```java
import java.io.*;

import javax.servlet.*;
import javax.servlet.http.*;

public abstract class RedirectingServlet
        extends HttpServlet
{
  protected HttpSession itsSession;
  protected HttpServletResponse itsResponse;
  protected HttpServletRequest itsRequest;
  public abstract void execute()
    throws ServletException,IOException;

  public void doGet(
          HttpServletRequest request,HttpServletResponse
              response)
            throws ServletException,IOException
  {
    itsSession=request.getSession(true);
    itsResponse=response;
    itsRequest=request;
    execute();
    redirect();
  }

  private void redirect()
          throws ServletException,IOException
  {
    String url=(String)itsRequest.getParameter("url");
    if(url==null)
      url=getInitParameter("home");
    itsResponse.sendRedirect(url);
  }

  protected void saveUserInSession(String userId)
  {
    itsSession.putValue("email",userId);
  }

  public void doPost(
          HttpServletRequest request,HttpServletResponse
              response)
            throws ServletException,IOException
```

```
   {
     doGet(request,response);
   }
 }
```

LISTING A.30 register.jsp

```
<HTML>
<HEAD>
<TITLE>
xpinpractice.com registration page
</TITLE>

<%@ include file="header.jsp" %>

<form method="POST" action="/servlet/register">
<TR>
<TD align=right width="255" height="34"> 
</TD>
<TD bgColor=#008080 width=4 height="34"> 
</TD>
<TD height="1" width="275">
<table cellpadding="4">
<tr>
<td>
<font face="arial, helvetica" size="2">
<b>
You must be a member to access this page.
</b>
</font>
</td>
</tr>
</table>
</TD>
</TR>
<%@ include file="row-space.jsp" %>
<TR>
<TD align=right width=255 height="34">
<font face="arial, helvetica" size="2">
<b>
Just visiting?  
</b>
```

Listing continued on next page.

```
</font>
</TD>
<TD bgColor=#008080 width=4 height="34">
<IMG border=0 height=1 src="images/spacer.gif" width=1>
</TD>
<TD height="34" width="275">
<IMG border=0 height=1 src="images/spacer.gif" width=2>
<FONT face="arial, helvetica" size=3>
<A href="/servlet/guest?url=<%=
request.getParameter("url") %>">
Guest
</A>
</FONT>
</TD>
</TR>
<%@ include file="row-space.jsp" %>
<TR>
<TD align=right width="255" height="34">
<p align="right">
<font face="arial, helvetica" size="2">
<b>
Already a member?   
</b>
</font>
</p>
</TD>
<TD bgColor=#008080 width=4 height="10">
<IMG border=0 height=1 src="images/spacer.gif" width=1>
</TD>
<TD height="34" width="275">
<IMG border=0 height=1 src="images/spacer.gif" width=2>
<FONT face="arial, helvetica" size=3>
<A href="/userproject/login.jsp?url=<%=
request.getParameter("url") %>">
Login!
</A>
</FONT>
</TD>
</TR>
<%@ include file="row-space.jsp" %>
<TR>
<TD align=right width=255 height="34">
<font face="arial, helvetica" size="2">
 
</font>
</TD>
```

```
<TD bgColor=#008080 width=4 height="34">
<IMG border=0 height=1 src="images/spacer.gif" width=1>
</TD>
<TD height="1" width="275">
<IMG border=0 height=1 src="images/spacer.gif" width=2>
<FONT face="arial, helvetica" size=2>
<b>
general information
</b>
</FONT>
</TD>
</TR>
<%@ include file="row-space.jsp" %>
<TR>
<TD align=right width=255 height="34">
<font face="arial, helvetica" size="2">
<b>
First name   
</b>
</font>
</TD>
<TD bgColor=#008080 width=4 height="34">
<IMG border=0 height=1 src="images/spacer.gif" width=1>
</TD>
<TD height="1" width="275">
<IMG border=0 height=1 src="images/spacer.gif" width=2>
<FONT face="arial, helvetica" size=3>
<INPUT type=text maxLength=100 name="firstname"></FONT>
</TD>
</TR>
<%@ include file="row-space.jsp" %>
<TR>
<TD align=right width=255 height="34">
<font face="arial, helvetica" size="2">
<b>
Last name   
</b>
</font>
</TD>
<TD bgColor=#008080 width=4 height="34">
<IMG border=0 height=1 src="images/spacer.gif" width=1>
</TD>
<TD height="1" width="275">
<IMG border=0 height=1 src="images/spacer.gif" width=2>
```

Listing continued on next page.

```
<FONT face="arial, helvetica" size=3>
<INPUT type=text maxLength=100 name="lastname"></FONT>
</TD>
</TR>
<%@ include file="row-space.jsp" %>
<TR>
<TD align=right width=255 height="34">
<font face="arial, helvetica" size="2">
<b>
Organization   
</b>
</font>
</TD>
<TD bgColor=#008080 width=4 height="34">
<IMG border=0 height=1 src="images/spacer.gif" width=1>
</TD>
<TD height="1" width="275">
<IMG border=0 height=1 src="images/spacer.gif" width=2>
<FONT face="arial, helvetica" size=3>
<INPUT type=text maxLength=100 name="organization"
size="30"></FONT>
</TD>
</TR>
<%@ include file="row-space.jsp" %>
<TR>
<TD align=right width=255 height="34">
<font face="arial, helvetica" size="2">
<b>
Add to mailing list?   
</b>
</font>
</TD>
<TD bgColor=#008080 width=4 height="34">
<IMG border=0 height=1 src="images/spacer.gif" width=1>
</TD>
<td>
<table>
<tr>
<TD>
<FONT face="arial, helvetica" size=3> 
<INPUT CHECKED name="notification"
type="checkbox" value="true">
</FONT>
</TD>
<td>
<FONT face="arial, helvetica" size=2>
```

```
We will send you notifications of new products and
services.
We will not sell your name to any other mailing list. We
promise!
</FONT>
</td>
</tr>
</table>
</td>
</TR>
<%@ include file="row-space.jsp" %>
<TR>
<TD align=right width=255 height="34">
<font face="arial, helvetica" size="2">
 
</font>
</TD>
<TD bgColor=#008080 width=4 height="34">
<IMG border=0 height=1 src="images/spacer.gif" width=1>
</TD>
<TD height="1" width="275">
<IMG border=0 height=1 src="images/spacer.gif" width=2>
<FONT face="arial, helvetica" size=2>
<b>
account access
</b>
</FONT>
</TD>
</TR>
<%@ include file="row-space.jsp" %>
<TR>
<TD align=right width=255 height="34">
<font face="arial, helvetica" size="2">
<b>
E-mail address   
</b>
</font>
</TD>
<TD bgColor=#008080 width=4 height="34">
<IMG border=0 height=1 src="images/spacer.gif" width=1>
</TD>
<TD height="1" width="275">
<IMG border=0 height=1 src="images/spacer.gif" width=2>
<FONT face="arial, helvetica" size=3>
```

Listing continued on next page.

```
<INPUT type=text maxLength=100 name="emailAddress"
size="30"></FONT>
</TD>
</TR>
<%@ include file="row-space.jsp" %>
<TR>
<TD align=right width=255 height="34">
<font face="arial, helvetica" size="2">
<b>
Password   
</b>
</font>
</TD>
<TD bgColor=#008080 width=4 height="25">
 
</TD>
<TD height="25" width="275">
<table cellpadding=3>
<tr>
<td>
<FONT face="arial, helvetica" size=2>
Your password will be emailed to you immediately
after you finish setting up your account.
</FONT>
</td>
</tr>
</table>
</TD>
</TR>
<%@ include file="row-space.jsp" %>
<TR>
<TD align=right width=255 height="34">
<font face="arial, helvetica" size="2">
<b>
Click here to read?  
</b>
</font>
</TD>
<TD bgColor=#008080 width=4 height="34">
<IMG border=0 height=1 src="images/spacer.gif" width=1>
</TD>
<TD height="34" width="275">
<IMG border=0 height=1 src="images/spacer.gif" width=2>
<FONT face="arial, helvetica" size=3>
```

```
<A href="/sitepolicies.html">
Site Policies
</A>
</FONT>
</TD>
</TR>
<%@ include file="row-space.jsp" %>
<TR>
<TD align=right width="255" height="34">
<p align="right">
<font face="arial, helvetica" size="2">
<b>
That's all . . .   
</b>
</font>
</p>
</TD>
<TD bgColor=#008080 width=4 height="34">
<IMG border=0 height=1 src="images/spacer.gif" width=1>
</TD>
<TD height="27" width="275">
<FONT face="arial, helvetica" size=3> </FONT>
<IMG border=0 height=1 src="images/spacer.gif" width=1>
<input type="submit" value="Register" name="register">
</TD>
</TR>
<input type=hidden name="url" value="<%=
request.getParameter("url") %>">
</FORM>
<%@ include file="row-space.jsp" %>
</TBODY>
</TABLE>

</BODY>
</HTML>
```

LISTING A.31 RegistrationAddFailure.jsp

```
<HTML>
<HEAD>
<TITLE>
Registration Add Failure
</TITLE>

<%@ include file="header.jsp" %>

<TR>
<TD align=right width="255" height="34"> 
</TD>
<TD bgColor=#008080 width=4 height="34"> 
</TD>
<TD height="1" width="275">
<TABLE cellpadding="3">
<TR>
<TD>
<font face="arial, helvetica" size="2">
<b>There was a problem adding: <%=
request.getParameter("email") %> to our database.</b>.
</font>
<font face="arial, helvetica, ms sans serif" size=2>
<p>
<a href="/userproject/register.jsp?url=<%=
request.getParameter("url") %>">
<b>
Click here to try again!
</b>
</a>
</p>
</font>
</TD>
</TR>
</TABLE>
</TD>
</TR>
<%@ include file="row-space.jsp" %>
</TBODY>
</TABLE>

</BODY>
</HTML>
```

LISTING A.32 RegistrationMailFailure.jsp

```
<HTML>
<HEAD>
<TITLE>
Registration Mail Failure.
</TITLE>

<%@ include file="header.jsp" %>

<TR>
<TD align=right width="255" height="34"> 
</TD>
<TD bgColor=#008080 width=4 height="34"> 
</TD>
<TD height="1" width="275">
<TABLE cellpadding="3">
<TR>
<TD>
<font face="arial, helvetica" size="2">
<b>There was a problem sending to: <%=
request.getParameter("email") %>, your account was not
added.</b>.
</font>
<font face="arial, helvetica, ms sans serif" size=2>
<p>
<a href="/userproject/register.jsp?url=<%=
request.getParameter("url") %>">
<b>
Click here to try again!
</b>
</a>
</p>
</font>
</TD>
</TR>
</TABLE>
</TD>
</TR>
<%@ include file="row-space.jsp" %>
</TBODY>
</TABLE>

</BODY>
</HTML>
```

```java
import java.io.*;

import javax.servlet.*;
import javax.servlet.http.*;

import com.oreilly.servlet.*;

public class RegistrationServlet extends HttpServlet
{
  private HttpServletRequest itsRequest;
  private HttpServletResponse itsResponse;
  private String email;
  public void doGet(
          HttpServletRequest request,HttpServletResponse
              response)
            throws ServletException,IOException
  {
    itsRequest=request;
    itsResponse=response;
    String firstName=itsRequest.getParameter("firstname");
    String lastName=itsRequest.getParameter("lastname");
    String organization=
      itsRequest.getParameter("organization");
    email=itsRequest.getParameter("emailAddress");
    String password=PasswordGenerator.generatePassword();
    boolean notify=true;
    String stringNotify=
      itsRequest.getParameter("notification");
    if(stringNotify==null)
      notify=false;
    User user=new User(email,password,firstName,lastName,
                       organization,notify);
    boolean success=UserDatabase.add(user);
    if(success){
      if(mailPassword(email,password))
        redirect("success");
      else{
        UserDatabase.delete(email);
        redirect("mailfailure");
      }
    }
    else{
      redirect("addfailure");
```

```java
    }
  }

  private boolean mailPassword(String email,
                              String password)
  {
    Mailer m=
      new SMTPMailer(getInitParameter("mail-server"));
    boolean wasSent=
      m.send(email,"Your Object Mentor Password",
             "Your Object Mentor Password is "+password);
    return wasSent;
  }

  private void redirect(String base)
         throws ServletException,IOException
  {
    String url=(String)itsRequest.getParameter("url");
    String baseURI=getInitParameter(base);
    String uri=baseURI+"?email="+email+"&url="+url;
    itsResponse.sendRedirect(uri);
  }

  private void redirect()
         throws ServletException,IOException
  {
    String url=(String)itsRequest.getParameter("url");
    if(url==null)
      url=getInitParameter("home");
    itsResponse.sendRedirect(url);
  }

  public void doPost(
         HttpServletRequest request,HttpServletResponse
             response)
           throws ServletException,IOException
  {
    doGet(request,response);
  }
}
```

LISTING A.34 RegistrationSuccess.jsp

```
<HTML>
<HEAD>
<TITLE>
Registration Success.
</TITLE>

<%@ include file="header.jsp" %>

<TR>
<TD align=right width="255" height="34"> 
</TD>
<TD bgColor=#008080 width=4 height="34"> 
</TD>
<TD height="1" width="275">
<TABLE cellpadding="3">
<TR>
<TD>
<font face="arial, helvetica" size="2">
<b>Your password was sent to: <%=
request.getParameter("email") %>.
It will be arriving shortly.</b>.
</font>
<font face="arial, helvetica, ms sans serif" size=2>
<p>
When your password arrives click
<a href="/userproject/login.jsp?url=<%=
request.getParameter("url") %>&email=<%=
request.getParameter("email") %>">
<b>here</b></a>
to login!
</p>
</font>
</TD>
</TR>
</TABLE>
</TD>
</TR>
<%@ include file="row-space.jsp" %>
</TBODY>
</TABLE>

</BODY>
</HTML>
```

LISTING A.35 ResetServlet.java

```java
import java.io.*;

import javax.servlet.*;
import javax.servlet.http.*;

public class ResetServlet extends HttpServlet
{
  public void doGet(
          HttpServletRequest request,HttpServletResponse
              response)
            throws ServletException,IOException
  {
    HttpSession s=request.getSession(true);
    s.invalidate();
    boolean found=false;
    Cookie[] cookies=request.getCookies();
    if(cookies!=null){
      for(int i=0;i<cookies.length&&!found;i++){
        Cookie c=cookies[i];
        String name=c.getName();
        String value=c.getValue();
        System.out.println("Cookie:"+name);
        if(name.equals("email")){
          found=true;
          c.setValue("");    // safety net when setMaxAge(0)
                                doesn't work.
          c.setMaxAge(-1);   // should work, but sometimes
                                doesn't.
          c.setPath("/");
          response.addCookie(c);
          return;
        }
      }
    }
    response.sendRedirect("/userproject/default.html");
  }

  public void doPost(
          HttpServletRequest request,HttpServletResponse
              response)
            throws ServletException,IOException
  {
    doGet(request,response);
  }
}
```

LISTING A.36 row-space.jsp

```
<TR>
<TD height="1" width="255">
<FONT face="arial, helvetica" size=2> </FONT>
<IMG border=0 height=1 src="images/spacer.gif" width=1>
</TD>
<TD bgColor=#C0C0C0 width=4 height="12">
<IMG border=0 height=1 src="images/spacer.gif" width=1>
</TD>
<TD height="1" width="275">
<FONT face="arial, helvetica" size=2> </FONT>
<IMG border=0 height=1 src="images/spacer.gif" width=1>
</TD>
</TR>
```

LISTING A.37 TestPasswordGenerator.java

```java
import junit.framework.*;

public class TestPasswordGenerator extends TestCase
{
  public TestPasswordGenerator(String name)
  {
    super(name);
  }

  public void testPasswordGenerator()
  {
    String password=PasswordGenerator.generatePassword();
    System.out.println("Password = "+password);
    assertEquals(8,password.length());
  }
}
```

Index

Release planning, *continued*
  second iteration, 139–141
  stories, current status, 144
  stories, first release, completed, 143
  stories, first release, planned, 142–143
  third iteration, 141–142
  velocity, 11, 31
  velocity, first iteration planning, 45
Reset Servlet task
  problems, 123–125
  time estimate, 42–43

S
Smart Site Header user story
  architectural significance, 30–31
  first release, original planning, 33
  first release, planned, 143
  high priority technical risk, 144–145
  origin, 19–20
  relationship with cookies, 125
Spikes, project exploration period, 10
Spoofing, 92–104
Stories. *See* user stories

T
Tasks
  breakdown of user stories, 36–42
  time estimates, 42–45
Testing, JUnit framework, 48–51
Transparent Login user story
  cookies, 70–74
  first release, original planning, 33

  first release, planned and completed, 143
  origin, 22
Triggering the Login Mechanism user story, origin, 15–16

U
User Registration user story
  first release, original planning, 33
  first release, planned and completed, 143
  origin, 23
User stories
  breaking down into tasks, 36–42
  defined, 9–10
  first release, planned compared to completed, 142–143
  prioritizing, 30
  task time estimates, 42–45
Username as E-mail Address user story
  origin, 16–17
  unique identifier, 23

V
Velocity, release planning, 11, 31
  first iteration planning, 45

W
Web sites
  user stories, Page Width, 26–27
  user stories, Smart Site Header, 19–20, 30–31, 33, 125, 144–145

X

XP projects. *See also* iterations;
    release planning
  communication, 148
  exploration period, 9–10
  feedback, 149
  lessons learned, 149–151

Lowell, miscommunication,
    130–134
Lowell, miscommunication,
    troubleshooting, 134–135
operating system architecture,
    18–19
pair programming, 12–13

The XP Series

Kent Beck, Series Advisor

Extreme Programming Explained
By Kent Beck
0201616416
Paperback
© 2000

The XP Manifesto

Planning Extreme Programming
By Kent Beck and Martin Fowler
0201710919
Paperback
© 2001

Planning Projects with XP

Extreme Programming Installed
By Ron Jeffries, Ann Anderson, and Chet Hendrickson
0201708426
Paperback
© 2001

Get XP Up and Running in Your Organization

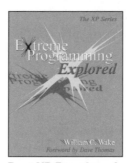

Extreme Programming Examined
By Giancarlo Succi and Michele Marchesi
0201710404
Paperback
© 2001

Best XP Practices as Presented and Analyzed at the recent Extreme Programming Conference

Extreme Programming in Practice
By James Newkirk and Robert C. Martin
0201709376
Paperback
© 2001

Learn from the Chronicle of an XP Project

Extreme Programming Explored
By William C. Wake
0201733978
Paperback
© 2002

Best XP Practices for Developers

Extreme Programming Applied
By Ken Auer and Roy Miller
0201616408
Paperback
© 2002

Delves Deeper into XP Theory

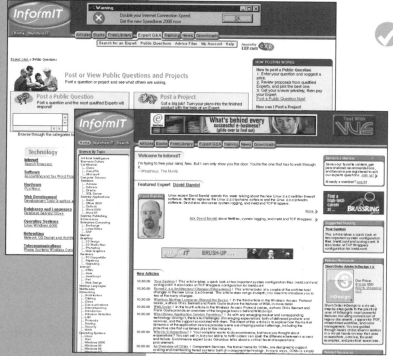

Register
Your Book
at www.aw.com/cseng/register

You may be eligible to receive:
- Advance notice of forthcoming editions of the book
- Related book recommendations
- Chapter excerpts and supplements of forthcoming titles
- Information about special contests and promotions throughout the year
- Notices and reminders about author appearances, tradeshows, and online chats with special guests

Contact us

If you are interested in writing a book or reviewing manuscripts prior to publication, please write to us at:

Editorial Department
Addison-Wesley Professional
75 Arlington Street, Suite 300
Boston, MA 02116 USA
Email: AWPro@aw.com

Addison-Wesley

Visit us on the Web: http://www.aw.com/cseng